The
Creative
Hostess

# HEART

OF THE

# COTSWOLDS

## COOKBOOK

2

We would like to thank all those who have helped us in the preparation of this book, particularly:
Joyce Barker, BA FSA,
and all the restaurateurs and chefs listed on pages 76-8 who have so kindly provided us with recipes.

"He builded better than he knew; –
The conscious stone to beauty grew."     The Problem
RALPH WALDO EMERSON, 1803-1882

First published 1982 by                           ISBN 0 904330 98 2
Marion Edwards Limited,    Second Impression, February 1983
10 Barley Mow Passage,              Printed in England by
London W4.                          T.J. Press (Padstow) Ltd.

The Creative Hostess

# HEART OF THE
# COTSWOLDS
## COOKBOOK

WITH DRAWINGS OF THE
VILLAGES AND COUNTRYSIDE
BY
GERALDINE MARCHAND

4

# *Introduction*

*"How sweet is the shepherd's sweet lot!*
*From the morn to the evening he strays;*
*He shall follow his sheep all the day,*
*And his tongue shall be filled with praise."*
                                    The Shepherd
                        WILLIAM BLAKE, 1757-1827

*We hope you will not need a shepherd to guide you to this Cotswolds recipe collection! In it you will find a wide cross-section of culinary creations served in restaurants and hotels in the very heart of the region, and tempting many a traveller to stray from his sight seeing! Ranging from the exotic to the quick and easy, the creative cooks and chefs have let us into the secrets of their many original recipes.*

*Take your time in the Cotswolds — there is much to see, and even more to be missed if you hurry through! As you wander around the sleepy little villages, keep your eyes open for fascinating details — in the pages which follow, we tell you about some of those we discovered on our travels.*

*Beautiful scenery and tired feet are guaranteed to give you a roaring (like a Cotswold lion?) appetite!*

*Enjoy this little memento at your leisure. Dip into its pages to discover more about this enchanting area, and impress your friends by re-creating at home some of the mouthwatering dishes of the region.*

## MORETON-IN-MARSH

The town takes its name from the fact that it stands on the boundary of three counties — marsh meaning boundary. Built on the Fosse Way, the main street is lined with buildings from the late 18th and early 19th centuries when the town was an important linen weaving centre, and a major stopping place for stage coaches. Charles I stayed at The White Hart in 1644. On the corner of Oxford Street stands the unique 16th century Curfew Tower, housing a bell dated 1633 which used to be rung whenever the town needed to summon the local fire brigade. The tower also contains the local lock-up!

# *Contents*

**Recipes**

**Historical Notes**

**A note on measures and conversions**
Ingredients are given in metric, Imperial and American measures. **Use measures from one column only.** Teaspoon and tablespoon measures in the metric column correspond to 5 ml and 15 ml respectively.

CHIPPING CAMPDEN PARISH CHURCH (overleaf)
Enter the church through an avenue of limes planted in 1770 in honour of the twelve Apostles. The 120 ft tower and walls 5 ft thick reflect the opulence which the town enjoyed at the peak of the wool trade. Look inside, and see the exquisite medieval embroidery which includes a 14th century cope and 15th century altar hangings. The late Queen Mary ordered that the altar frontal in Westminster Abbey should be copied from these for use at George V's coronation.

# About the Cotswolds

Rolling landscapes and golden, weathered stone form the essence of scenery in that part of the heart of England which we know as the Cotswolds. Situated mainly in Gloucestershire, it also extends into Avon and Wiltshire, Oxfordshire, Warwickshire and Worcestershire.

## How the Cotswolds got their name

The Cotswolds owe their name to Saxon farmers, the word 'cote' meaning sheepfold and 'wold' meaning downs. But although they gave the area the name by which we know it today, the Saxons were not the first to occupy it. Monuments dating from about 4000 BC, now lie covered with grass and long barrows, such as Belas Knapp and Hetty Pegler's Tump, were originally constructed as multiple tombs. Evidence of Bronze Age settlements is also present in monuments such as the Rollright Stones.

## The coming of the Romans

The Roman town of Corinium (now Cirencester), was second in size only to London, and sited at the junction of five roads, the most famous being the Fosse Way, running through Moreton-in-Marsh and on to Bath.

Both the straight roads that still criss-cross the Cotswolds today, and the mosaic pavements which have been uncovered by farmers' ploughs, date from the Roman occupation. Judging by the luxurious villas which have been unearthed, it seems many of these colonials enjoyed an affluent lifestyle; although evidence has been found of more modest farmhouses.

## The early sheep farmers

The Saxons who followed after the departure of the Romans were the first to rear sheep in any number. By the Middle Ages, farmers were breeding long-wooled sheep known as 'Cotswold lions'. Although now a rare breed, they can still be seen at the Cotswold Farm Park.

## The Civil War

The Civil War of 1642 brought unrest to this peaceful area, the merchants being particularly unfriendly to the Monarch as he commandeered their cloth to make uniforms for his soldiers! Charles I made his headquarters at Oxford, so the Cotswolds witnessed many scenes of conflict between Cromwell, with his New Model Army, and the Royalists.

Today, battles of the Civil War are re-created by members of The Sealed Knot Society, who take their warring very seriously, wearing beautiful uniforms and using weapons modelled on the originals. Their enthusiasm is such that real casualties are not uncommon!

## The character of the Cotswolds

Being formed by a great slab of oolitic limestone, the Cotswolds had a ready supply of excellent building material. The builders of the area developed the distinctive Cotswold style — mullioned windows, prominent gables and stone-tiled roofs — which complements the scenery so well.

Built without the use of earth or mortar and also made from local limestone, drystone walls are another of the area's most distinctive features. They first became common in the 18th century when the ancient open-field system was replaced by the enclosure of agricultural land.

CHIPPING CAMPDEN ALMSHOUSES AND PARISH CHURCH
Walk up these ancient Cotswold steps to view the almshouses built by the first Viscount Campden, Sir Baptist Hicks, whose immense wealth led James I to borrow from him! Beyond may be seen the tower of the impressive parish church (see page 5).

*"Beauty is like a rich stone, best plain set."*
Essays, "Of Beauty"
FRANCIS BACON, 1561-1626

## CHIPPING CAMPDEN

This attractive town nestles in the hollow beneath Dover's Hill – once the home of the most prosperous Cotswold wool merchants. The word 'Chipping' means market. This 17th century market hall, built by Sir Baptist Hicks (see p.7) was once a vital and thriving part of the community.

The original manor house where he lived had a transparent dome which he lit at night to guide travellers on the Wold. Sadly, it was burnt down by the Royalists to prevent its capture. The fifteenth century church contains some excellent brasses.

## GLOUCESTER CHEESE SOUP                    *Serves 8*

This regional recipe from the Fleece Inn is rich, colourful and satisfying. Set in the market place at Cirencester — often called the capital of the Cotswolds — the hotel is well named in a town originally made rich by the wool trade. It was a meeting place for flockmasters and wool staplers.

| Metric | | lb/oz | U.S.A. |
|---|---|---|---|
| 60 g | Of each of the following chopped, fresh vegetables: Leeks, carrots, turnips, celery, onions, potatoes | 2 oz | ½ cup |
| 60 g | Butter | 2 oz | ¼ cup |
| 30 g | Flour | 1 oz | ¼ cup |
| 1.25 litres | Chicken stock | 2 pt | 5 cups |
| | Bouquet garni | | |
| 175 g | Double Gloucester cheese, grated | 6 oz | 1 ½ cups |
| 200 ml | Cream | 4 tbsp | ½ cup |
| | To serve: | | |
| 4 | Slices of bread, cut into croûtons and toasted | 4 | 4 |
| | Chopped parsley | | |

DOUBLE GLOUCESTER CHEESE, made from the milk of Old Gloucester cattle, is so-called because the milk has to be processed twice. Dating from the 14th century, this breed has been preserved at Cotswold Farm Park along with a type of pig called the Gloucester Old Spot, once known as the orchard pig because it could live off windfalls. The Duke of Beaufort encouraged his tenants to keep these pigs because they never panicked when his hounds chased through their grazing grounds!

1. Clean and prepare the vegetables.
2. Melt the butter in a pan and gently cook the vegetables for about 20 minutes until tender but not coloured.
3. Stir in the flour and mix thoroughly with the vegetables. Continue to cook gently for 10 minutes.
4. Pour in the stock, stirring continuously. Add the bouquet garni, season to taste and bring to the boil.
5. Add two-thirds of the cheese and simmer gently for an hour.
6. Pass the soup through a fine strainer. Check the seasoning, adding more salt and pepper if required.
7. Re-heat the soup, remove from the heat and stir in the cream.
8. Pour into warm bowls, top each one with a handful of croûtons, sprinkle with the remaining cheese, and garnish with chopped parsley. Serve immediately.

TRUE DOUBLE GLOSTER CHEESE from the milk of Gloster cows is sold regularly in Cirencester Town Market.

## SAFFRON SOUP                                                   *Serves 8*

Chef Hill of the famous Lygon Arms in Broadway has provided this colourful and delicious contribution.

| Metric |  | lb/oz | U.S.A. |
|---|---|---|---|
| 1 kg | Leeks | 2 lb | 2 lb |
| 500 g | Onions | 1 lb | 1 lb |
| 250 g | Celery | 8 oz | ½ lb |
| 1 kg | Potatoes, peeled | 2 lb | 2 lb |
| 1.25 litres | Chicken stock | 2 pt | 5 cups |
| 1 tsp | Saffron | ½ oz | 1 tsp |
| 1 | Mixed herbs, pinch of | 1 | 1 |
| 150 ml | Double cream | ¼ pt | ½ cup |
| 2 | Lemons, cut into wedges | 2 | 2 |

1. Clean and trim the vegetables and cut into 2-3 cm (1") long pieces.
2. Put the stock in a large saucepan with the saffron, mixed herbs and vegetables and bring to the boil.
3. Simmer for about an hour or until the potatoes are tender, then pass through a sieve or blend in a liquidiser.
4. Return to the pan and heat through. Stir in the cream and serve with lemon wedges.

NANCY MITFORD used the Jacobean manor at Asthall near Burford as the setting for her satirical novel 'The Pursuit of Love'. Today, the authoress's grave lies alongside that of her sister Unity in Swinbrook parish (Footnote!) churchyard.

Deep fried mushrooms are a popular starter in the Cotswolds – we received several recipes for them. It's hard to say which one is best – we recommend them all!

## NORWEGIAN BAKED MUSHROOMS                    Serves 4

The Royalist Hotel dates back to 900 AD and is believed to be the oldest building in Stow-on-the-Wold. This recipe is a favourite with visitors all the year round.

| Metric | | lb/oz | U.S.A. |
|---|---|---|---|
| 250 g | Mushrooms, sliced | 8 oz | 2½ cups |
| 30 g | Butter | 1 oz | 2 tbsp |
| 60 g | Medium onion, finely chopped | 2 oz | ½ cup |
| 1 tsp | Mixed herbs | 1 tsp | 1 tsp |
| 150 ml | Sour cream | ¼ pt | ½ cup |
| 2 tbsp | White wine | 2 tbsp | 2 tbsp |
| 4 tbsp | Cheese, grated | 4 tbsp | ⅓ cup |

1. Set the oven to 180°C, 350°F, Gas Mark 4.
2. Melt the butter in a pan and add the onion. Sauté until transparent but not browned.
3. Add the mushrooms and mixed herbs, and cook gently until the mushrooms are tender.
4. Stir in the sour cream and white wine. Season to taste.
5. Butter four ramekin dishes and divide the mixture equally between them. Sprinkle the tops with grated cheese.
6. Bake for 20 minutes until the cheese is bubbling. Serve immediately.

## MUSHROOMS ABBOTT                    Serves 8

The deep colour and rich flavour of double Gloucester cheese adds a nice local touch to this recipe from the White Hart at Chipping Norton.

| Metric | | lb/oz | U.S.A. |
|---|---|---|---|
| 500 g | Large flat mushrooms | 1 lb | 1 lb |
| 125 g | Double Gloucester cheese | 4 oz | ¼ lb |
| 2 tbsp | Flour | 2 tbsp | ¼ cup |
| 1 | Egg, beaten | 1 | 1 |
| 8 tbsp | Fresh breadcrumbs | 8 tbsp | ⅔ cup |
| | Oil for frying | | |
| | To serve: | | |
| | Tartare sauce | | |

1. Wash the mushrooms and remove the stems (reserving for use in soups or casseroles).
2. Fill the mushrooms with slices of cheese, and coat all over with flour.

3. Brush the mushrooms with the beaten egg and roll in the breadcrumbs.
4. Heat the oil and deep fry the mushrooms until golden. Drain on kitchen paper.
5. Place on a warm dish and serve with tartare sauce.

## ATTEREAU OF TONGUE AND MUSHROOMS    *Serves 8*

William Morris described Bibury as "the most delightful village in England". This deep fried delicacy from the Swan Hotel, Bibury is one of the most tasty appetizers on offer in the Cotswolds. You will need eight small skewers.

| Metric | | lb/oz | U.S.A. |
|---|---|---|---|
| 250 g | 24 Button mushrooms | 8-10 oz | 24 |
| 500 g | Ox tongue | 1 lb | 1 lb |
| 600 ml | Béchamel sauce | 1 pt | 2 cups |
| | (see p.31, but make a double quantity) | | |
| 2 tbsp | Dry sherry | 2 tbsp | 2 tbsp |
| 2 | Egg yolks | 2 | 2 |
| 250 g | Fresh breadcrumbs | 8 oz | 4 cups |
| | Oil for frying | | |
| 4 tbsp | Parsley, chopped | 4 tbsp | ⅓ cup |
| 300 ml | Madeira sauce | ½ pt | 1 cup |

1. Make the béchamel sauce. Leave to cool and thicken.
2. Wash the mushrooms and cut the stalks back to the rim. Cut out 16 tongue rounds approximately the same size as the mushrooms.
3. Put 3 mushrooms and 2 pieces of tongue on each skewer, alternating them.
4. Add the sherry and egg yolks to the sauce and mix well.
5. Dip each attereau into the sauce then roll in the breadcrumbs until completely coated. Refrigerate for about an hour before cooking. Make the Madeira sauce.
6. Deep fry in the oil until golden brown. Drain on kitchen paper then place each attereau on a plate. Pull out the skewer, sprinkle with chopped parsley, and serve with hot Madeira sauce.

### Madeira sauce

| Metric | | lb/oz | U.S.A. |
|---|---|---|---|
| 150 ml | Madeira | ¼ pt | ½ cup |
| 250 g | Mushrooms, chopped | 4 oz | 1 cup |
| 150 ml | Cream | ¼ pt | ½ cup |

1. Pour the Madeira into a pan and add the mushrooms.
2. Cook for a few minutes then add the cream. Stir until the sauce has thickened and reduced.

## POTTED STILTON CREAM WITH WALNUTS    *Serves 4-6*

An old English dish from a fascinating half-timbered hotel at Moreton-in-Marsh. The White Hart Royal Hotel was visited by Charles I in 1644, and parts of it date back to the fifteenth century.

| *Metric* | | *lb/oz* | *U.S.A.* |
|---|---|---|---|
| 150 ml | *Double cream* | ¼ pt | ½ cup |
| ⅓ | *Lemon, juice of* | ⅓ | ⅓ |
| 125 g | *Stilton, crumbled* | 4 oz | 1 cup |
| | To garnish: | | |
| | *Walnut halves, chopped* | | |
| | *    parsley and strips of celery* | | |

1. Lightly whip the double cream, season with salt and pepper and add the lemon juice.
2. Crumble the Stilton and blend with the cream. Mix well.
3. Check the seasoning. Transfer to ramekin dishes and place in the refrigerator to set.
4. Serve garnished with halved walnuts, chopped parsley and rough cut strips of celery.

IN THE HALL OF THE HOTEL, look out for an interesting old map showing the London to Aberystwyth road which still runs t'ough the town.

## HOT MOUSSE OF VEGETABLES
## WITH HAZELNUT SAUCE    *Serves 8*

A pretty vegetarian starter from The Rafters in Stow-on-the-Wold.

| *Metric* | | *lb/oz* | *U.S.A.* |
|---|---|---|---|
| 750 g | *Carrots, chopped* | 1 ½ lb | 6 cups |
| 1 kg | *Celeriac, peeled and* | 2 lb | 2 lb |
| | *    quartered* | | |
| 1.25 kg | *Fresh spinach, washed* | 2 ½ lb | 2 ½ lb |
| | *    and destalked* | | |
| 1 tsp | *Sugar* | 1 tsp | 1 tsp |
| 2 tsp | *Lemon juice* | 2 tsp | 2 tsp |
| 30 g | *Butter* | 1 oz | 2 tbsp |
| 1 | *Fresh thyme, pinch of* | 1 | 1 |
| 1 | *Mixed herbs, pinch of* | 1 | 1 |
| 3 | *Egg yolks* | 3 | 3 |
| 3 | *Eggs* | 3 | 3 |

1. Cover the carrots with water, add a little salt and sugar and cook until tender.
2. Cover the celeriac with water, add a little salt and the lemon juice and cook until tender. The liquor from these two vegetables is to be used in the sauce, having been well reduced, so do not add too much salt.

3. Plunge the spinach into boiling water and cook until tender.

4. Keeping the vegetables separate, drain well, reserving the liquor. Return each vegetable to its pan, add a small knob of butter to each and place on a low heat to dry out.

5. Season the carrots with thyme, the spinach with mixed herbs, and all three with salt and pepper to taste.

6. Purée the carrots, with one egg yolk, in a food processor or liquidiser. Liquidise for a minute then add one whole egg and process for another minute. Remove the carrots and repeat with the spinach and the celeriac.

7. Set the oven to 180°C, 350°F, Gas Mark 4, then well grease a small rectangular cake tin or eight individual moulds.

8. Layer the purées, with the celeriac between each layer, into the mould. Cover with tin foil and place in a large roasting pan with enough water to come half way up the sides of the tin or moulds.

9. Bring to the boil on the stove then place in the oven until the mousse is just set. The timing will depend on the depth of the mixture in the mould – about 15 minutes for individual moulds but at least 30 minutes for the cake tin.

10. Remove from the oven and leave to stand for 15 minutes before turning out.

11. Serve sliced on a warm serving dish with the sauce underneath, similarly for the individual moulds.

*The mousse may be made in advance and re-heated in a water bath.*

## Hazelnut sauce

| Metric | | lb/oz | U.S.A. |
|---|---|---|---|
| 125 g | Hazelnuts | 4 oz | 1 cup |
| 350 g | Unsalted butter | 12 oz | 1 ½ cups |
| 150 ml | White wine | ¼ pt | ½ cup |
| 150 ml | Vegetable liquor | ¼ pt | ½ cup |
| 150 ml | Double cream | ¼ pt | ½ cup |
| | Lemon juice | | |

1. Toast the hazelnuts under the grill, then remove the skins and chop the nuts finely.

2. Beat the butter and mix in the hazelnuts. Place in the refrigerator to set.

3. Place the wine and vegetable liquor in a tall sided pan and boil to reduce the quantity until you have about one tablespoon in all.

4. Stir in the cream and bring to the boil. When the cream is boiling rapidly, add all the cold hazelnut butter and continue boiling until all the butter is incorporated.

5. Immediately add one tablespoon cold water and a squeeze of lemon juice.

6. Season to taste. Keep warm but not too hot or the mixture will separate. Use as soon as possible.

## SALSIFY PASTIES
*Makes 8*

These subtly flavoured pastry parcels from the Broadway
Hotel make an unusual starter. They will cook to perfection
while you enjoy a pre-dinner drink.

| Metric | | lb/oz | U.S.A. |
|---|---|---|---|
| 350 g | Salsify | 12 oz | ¾ lb |
| 300 ml | Velouté sauce | ½ pt | 1 cup |
| 225 g | Puff pastry, home-made or frozen | 8 oz | ½ lb |
| 1 | Egg, beaten | 1 | 1 |

1. Make the velouté sauce.
2. Trim each stalk of the salsify and wash thoroughly under
   cold water. Scrape the stalks and cut into 2-3 cm (1")
   lengths. As each stalk is prepared, drop it into a bowl of
   cold water containing a drop of vinegar to prevent the
   stalks from turning brown.
3. Drain the salsify and place in a pan of boiling water. Cook
   for 20 minutes or until the stalks are tender, then drain.
   Place the salsify in a bowl and stir in the velouté sauce.
   Allow to cool.
4. Roll out the puff pastry and cut into rings with a large
   scone cutter.
5. Place 1 tbsp of salsify mixture on each circle.
6. Brush the edges of the pastry with egg, fold over and press
   the edges together to seal.
7. Brush the top of the pastry with egg, then bake in a
   moderate oven, 190°C, 375°F, Gas Mark 5, for 10-15
   minutes until the pastry is golden brown.

**Velouté sauce**
*Makes approx. 300 ml (½ pt)*

| Metric | | lb/oz | U.S.A. |
|---|---|---|---|
| 30 g | Butter | 1 oz | 2 tbsp |
| 60 g | Mushrooms, chopped | 2 oz | ¾ cup |
| 6 | Peppercorns | 6 | 6 |
| 1 tbsp | Parsley, chopped | 1 tbsp | 1 tbsp |
| 2 tbsp | Flour | 2 tbsp | 2 tbsp |
| 300 ml | Chicken stock | ½ pt | 1 cup |
| 1 tsp | Lemon juice | 1 tsp | 1 tsp |
| 3 tbsp | Single cream | 3 tbsp | ¼ cup |

1. Melt the butter in a pan and add the mushrooms,
   peppercorns and parsley. Cook gently for 10 minutes.
2. Stir in the flour and cook for a few minutes without
   browning until the flour is cooked.
3. Gradually add the stock, stirring all the time.
4. Simmer gently for one hour, then strain through a fine
   sieve. Season to taste and add the lemon juice.
5. Return to the pan and bring almost to boiling point.
   Remove from the heat and stir in the cream.

## HIDCOTE MANOR GARDEN, HIDCOTE BARTRIM

These magnificent gardens east of Chipping Campden were no more than a windswept site containing a fine cedar and a group of beeches at the beginning of the century. Transformed by Major Lawrence Johnston, they contain many botanical rarities. The gardens are open daily for the public's enjoyment, April to October, except Tuesdays and Fridays.

## MELON MADAME DRUMMOND HAY                                    Serves 4

This recipe from the Old Manse Hotel, Bourton-on-the-Water, is for a sauce which may be served with all types of melon. It can be served mixed with a Parisienne (small balls of melon) as a cocktail or with a melon half or slice served separately.

| Metric | | lb/oz | U.S.A. |
|--------|--------------------------------|-------|--------|
| 225 g | Redcurrant jelly | 8 oz | ⅔ cup |
| 2 tbsp | Kirsch | 2 tbsp | 2 tbsp |
| 2 tbsp | Port | 2 tbsp | 2 tbsp |
| 125 g | Stem ginger (cut into fine strips) | 4 oz | ⅓ cup |

1. Place all the ingredients in a small pan.
2. Simmer for 10 minutes stirring all the time.
3. Allow to cool and place in the refrigerator until needed.

## CURRIED PEARS                                    *Serves 4*

An unusual and inexpensive hot fruit first course from the Broadway Hotel.

| Metric | | lb/oz | U.S.A |
|--------|--------------------------------|-------|-------|
|        | 4 Large firm pears (canned may be used) | | |
| 1 tsp  | Curry powder                   | 1 tsp | 1 tsp |
| 1 tbsp | Brandy                         | 1 tbsp| 1 tbsp|
| 150 ml | Double cream                   | ¼ pt  | ½ cup |

1. Peel, halve and core the pears and simmer in slightly salted water for 10 minutes or until tender, then drain. (If using canned pears, drain well, but do not cook.)
2. Replace the pears in the pan and sprinkle with the curry powder. Pour over the brandy and flambé.
3. Add the cream. Cook gently until thick, but do not boil.
4. Place the pears on a warmed serving dish and coat with the sauce. Serve immediately.

## BRANDIED CHICKEN LIVERS WITH
## ORANGES AND CREAM                                *Serves 4*

A rich but easy-to-prepare appetizer for a special occasion from the Kings Arms Hotel, Chipping Campden.

| Metric | | lb/oz | U.S.A. |
|--------|--------------------------------|-------|--------|
| 225 g  | Chicken livers, chopped        | 8 oz  | 1 cup  |
| 30 g   | Clarified butter*              | 1 oz  | 2 tbsp |
|        | Brandy, to taste               | | |
| 1      | Orange, grated rind and juice  | 1     | 1      |
| 150 ml | Double cream                   | ¼ pt  | ½ cup  |

1. Melt the butter in a heavy pan and sauté the livers briskly.
2. When browned, add the brandy and flambé. Cook for 30 seconds over a high heat to reduce the liquid.
3. Lower the heat and stir in the rind and juice of the orange. Add the cream and cook gently, stirring all the time until you have a thick creamy consistency.
4. Season to taste with a pinch of salt and some ground black pepper and serve immediately.

*\*To clarify butter, melt over a gentle heat, without browning, until bubbling stops. Set aside until the milky solids settle. Skim the surface of the liquid and discard. Refrigerate until needed – Editor.*

THE DOVER GAMES, founded by Captain Robert Dover, were first held at Chipping Campden as a protest against Puritanism. A 17th century version of the Olympic Games, they included the rural sport of shin kicking! Today the games take place annually on the Friday following spring bank holiday.

### THE SHEEP SHEARER

The first stage in making woollen cloth is the shearing of the sheep. Now a highly mechanised art, the old shearers worked entirely with hand tools. The medieval Cotswold sheep produced only 1½ lb wool, but the variety reared at the turn of the century produced 8 lb.

# A Wealth of Wool

The wealth of the Cotswolds, obvious from the magnificent stone buildings throughout the area, has been derived from wool. The undulating terrain proved ideal for sheep-grazing and the first wool merchants emerged during the 14th century, making their fortunes as middlemen.

Wool was responsible for bringing great prosperity to the area and by the end of the 14th century it was the most important industry in England. Edward III even commanded that the most important man in the House of Lords — the Lord Chancellor — should sit on a woolsack as a reminder of the importance of the wool trade.

### An international trade

All wool for export had to pass through a fixed market, or staple, which was situated at Calais, so work for wool-brokers was plentiful. A century later, woven cloth became subject to import controls, so attention was turned to making cloth instead of simply exporting wool.

### The independent craftsman

Craftsmen were self-employed and worked individually — a spinner would sell wool to a weaver who in turn sold the woven cloth to a fuller. It was finally passed to a finisher before being sold to merchant tailors.

### CARDING THE WOOL

The wool was combed or 'carded' by hand, often by children. This involved stranding it backwards and forwards between two wire-pronged brushes.

THE SPINNER

Spinning was traditionally women's work, and the hum of the spinning wheel was a familiar sound in cottages throughout the land. Strong thread was needed for the long cloth warp, which had to be spun standing up.

## The emergence of the mills

The entrepreneurs were soon to appear! The clothier bought wool in bulk, farmed it out to spinners and weavers, then organised a factory for fulling, dyeing and finishing, finally selling the cloth.

## The wealth of the merchants

The clothiers' success is reflected in the magnificent churches and huge houses which they left behind. On merchants' tombs, the effigy can often be seen to have his feet resting on a woolsack or sheep instead of the traditional dog!

AT FAIRFORD, visit the magnificent wool church and see an example of medieval male chauvinism — the stained glass windows depict all the damned as women!

## Uley blue and Staffordshire scarlet

One example of a fine merchant's house is Gatcombe Park, bought by the Queen for Princess Anne and Captain Mark Phillips. It was built by Edward Sheppard of Uley, who was the largest manufacturer of Uley Blue cloth. Along with Stroudwater Scarlet, this was bought in bulk to clothe the children of charity schools all over the country — known as Bluecoat and Redcoat schools. A much-felted and virtually waterproofed fawn version of the cloth was worn by Parliamentarian soldiers, while the King's regiments sported Stroudwater Scarlet.

AT THE TURN OF THE CENTURY designer William Morris led a movement of craftsmen based in the Cotswolds. He fell in love with the local landscape and together with his friend, the painter Rossetti, he bought Kelmscot Manor near Lechlade, (although rumour has it that Rossetti was more attracted by Morris's wife than the countryside!).

## THE WEAVERS

The weaving was mostly done by men — you may recall that in "A Midsummer Night's Dream" the much teased Bottom was one. In the Cotswolds, broadlooms were used which needed two highly skilled weavers to throw the shuttle. The weavers' importance sadly declined with the introduction of the flying shuttle.

"Now I am a bachelor, I live by myself and I work at the weaving trade,
And the only thing that I ever did wrong,
Was to woo a fair young maid."

Weaver's Song
ANON

## THE FULLERS AND FINISHERS

Woven cloth was washed by fullers to shrink and thicken it, then dyed. This was a gruelling task. Great cauldrons were used, and the wet cloth often took several men to lift it.
The finisher trod the material in an alkaline solution.

## THE CLOTH DRESSER

Also known as the cropper or cutter, the cloth dresser was the last craftsman in the chain.

22

## ST EDWARD'S CAFE, STOW

Worth noting whilst wandering around Stow is St. Edward's house, an unusual old building with Corinthian pillars, originally the home of a wealthy wool merchant.

## The Industrial Revolution

By the end of the 18th century the wool industry had remained almost unchanged for 400 years. Suddenly, traditional methods began to be threatened by machinery. The spinning Jenny put an end to cottage spinning, while weavers' livelihoods were threatened by the flying shuttle. Workers fought violently against the introduction of new machinery, many self-employed individuals forming themselves into societies, later to become known as unions.

## The decline of trade

By the 1880s only large businesses could survive, both because of competition from Europe and a tax levied on wool.

SIR EDWARD ELGAR was inspired to write 'Introduction and Allegro for Strings' after a visit to the Cotswold Way — 100 miles of walking in beautiful landscape (we assume he didn't walk the whole way!)

Workers who had fought hard to maintain their independence could no longer make ends meet, and the end of the century saw the last of the old home weavers. With the demise of the wool trade, the Cotswolds declined. With only a brief respite during coaching days the area entered a period of depression and became a remote rural backwater, remaining so until recent times. It is ironic that this period of recession probably prevented money being spent on "modernising" (and probably ruining) many of today's beautiful homes and churches.

## EN ROUTE TO STOW

Stow-on-the-Wold-where-the-wind-blows-cold; at 700 ft above sea level, this is a most accurate description! This windswept town was once renowned throughout Europe for its fairs, which on one occasion, according to Defoe, included the sale of 20,000 sheep. The fair is still held but now centres around horses and equipment, not sheep. Stow is also famous for the 3,000 Royalist troops who fought the final battle of the Civil War just a mile out of the town. As the losers of the battle they were promptly imprisoned by Cromwell in Stow's large 12th century church!

THE MARKET SQUARE, STOW-ON-THE-WOLD (see page 29)

## ISLAND HOUSE PRAWN COCKTAIL                          *Serves 4*

Throughout winter, log fires greet visitors to this small
Chipping Campden restaurant in a house dating from 1673.
This quick and easy, fruity prawn cocktail is a refreshing
variation on an old favourite.

| Metric | | lb/oz | U.S.A. |
|---|---|---|---|
| 250 g | Shelled prawns | 8 oz | 1 cup |
| 4 | Lettuce leaves, shredded | 4 | 4 |
| 4 | Pineapple rings, cut in pieces | 4 | 4 |
| 2 | Bananas | 2 | 2 |
| | For the sauce: | | |
| 300 ml | Mayonnaise or salad cream | ½ pt | 1 cup |
| 3 tbsp | Tomato ketchup | 3 tbsp | ¼ cup |
| 1 tsp | Curry powder | 1 tsp | 1 tsp |
| 3 | Worcestershire sauce, dashes of | 3 | 3 |
| 1 tbsp | Lemon juice | 1 tbsp | 1 tbsp |
| | To garnish: | | |
| | Cucumber and tomato slices, and lemon wedges | | |

1. Prepare the sauce first by mixing all the ingredients
   together.
2. Divide the lettuce between four side plates and top with
   pineapple. Slice the bananas over the pineapple. Arrange
   the prawns on top and spoon over the sauce.
3. Decorate each plate with the garnishes.

## COLD SALMON AND NUT ROLL                          *Serves 6-8*

The complementary flavours of nuts and cream cheese are
effectively combined with salmon in this creative recipe from
the Old New Inn, Bourton-on-the-Water.

| Metric | | lb/oz | U.S.A. |
|---|---|---|---|
| 500 g | Fresh salmon, cooked* | 1 lb | 1 lb |
| 225 g | Smooth cream cheese | 8 oz | 1 cup |
| 1 tbsp | Shallots, finely chopped | 1 tbsp | 1 tbsp |
| 1 tbsp | Horseradish, grated | 1 tbsp | 1 tbsp |
| 1 tbsp | Lemon juice | 1 tbsp | 1 tbsp |
| 125 g | Pecans or walnuts, finely chopped | 4 oz | 1⅓ cups |
| 3 tbsp | Fresh green herbs, finely chopped | 3 tbsp | ⅓ cup |

1. To prepare the fresh salmon, remove any skin and bones then flake the fish. If using canned salmon, drain and flake the fish. Place in a bowl and beat well with the cream cheese, shallots and horseradish. Season well with salt and pepper, and add the lemon juice.
2. Shape the mixture into a roll, flatten the ends and chill in the refrigerator.
3. Mix the nuts and herbs well and spread on a large piece of foil.
4. Roll the salmon in the nut mixture until it is completely coated. Wrap in the foil and chill until required.
5. Cut into slices and serve with a green salad and toast.

*Canned may be used if fresh is not available.*

*"We are waiting for the long-promised invasion.*
*So are the fishes."*      Broadcast to the French People, 1940
WINSTON CHURCHILL, 1874-1965

## PATINA DE PISCIS FRICTA
## PATINA OF FRIED HERRING                        *Serves 2*

Fish and egg flavours combine effectively in this unusual offering from the King's Head Hotel, Cirencester.

| Metric | | lb/oz | U.S.A. |
|---|---|---|---|
| | 2 Herrings, gutted and trimmed | | |
| 2 | Eggs, lightly beaten | 2 | 2 |
| | Liquamen* | | |
| 1 tbsp | Wine oil | 1 tbsp | 1 tbsp |

1. Wash the herrings and dip in the egg until well coated.
2. Pour the liquamen and wine oil into a shallow pan and bring to the boil, then add the fish.
3. When the egg has set and the fish cooked on the under-side, turn them over carefully and cook on the other side.
4. Remove the fish to a serving dish. Pour over the oenogarum (pan juices), sprinkle with salt and pepper, and serve immediately.

*Liquamen is a fermented fish stock — if the real thing is not available, use 1 tbsp Tamara (readily available in Indian shops) mixed with 2 tsp of anchovy essence.*

*"Ann, Ann!*
*Come! as quick as you can!*
*There's a fish that talks*
*In the frying pan."*                        Alas, Alack
WALTER DE LA MARE, 1873-1956

## FISH QUENELLES WITH LOBSTER SAUCE        *Serves 12*

Next time you indulge in the extravagance of buying lobster or crab, save the shells and a little flesh to make this speciality created by Chef Llewellyn of the Swan Hotel at Bibury.

| Metric | | lb/oz | U.S.A. |
|---|---|---|---|
| 700 g | Whiting or haddock | 1½ lb | 1½ lb |
| | Greaseproof paper and crushed ice | | |
| 1 | Egg white, whisked | 1 | 1 |
| | For the panada: | | |
| 60 g | Butter | 2 oz | ¼ cup |
| 150 g | Flour | 5 oz | 1 cup |

1. To make the panada, put 300 ml (½ pt, 1 cup) of water, a pinch of salt and the butter into a pan and bring to the boil.
2. Remove from the heat, then add all the flour at once, stir well with a wooden spoon and return to the heat, drying and thickening the panada by stirring continuously. Remove from the heat.
3. Butter a sheet of greaseproof paper, spread the panada on it, and leave to cool.
4. Remove the skin and bones from the fish and sprinkle with a pinch of salt. Pound the flesh to a cream. Put into a mixer and whisk in the egg white. When thoroughly mixed, add the cold panada and mix again. Wrap this mixture in greaseproof paper and lay on crushed ice for 1 hour.
5. Using two dessertspoons (tablespoons USA), make egg-shaped quenelles. Poach them in boiling salted water for about 10 minutes.
6. When cooked, remove, drain, and transfer to hot plates. Serve with lobster sauce.

**Lobster sauce**                                     *Serves 12*

| Metric | | lb/oz | U.S.A. |
|---|---|---|---|
| 60 g | Lobster meat | 2 oz | ⅓ cup |
| 250 g | Lobster shells | 8 oz | ½ lb |
| 125 g | Butter | 4 oz | ½ cup |
| 2 | Shallots or button onions, chopped | 2 | ½ cup |
| 1 | Bay leaf | 1 | 1 |
| 125 g | Flour | 4 oz | 1 cup |
| 10 ml | Tomato purée | 2 tsp | 2 tsp |
| 1.25 litres | Fish stock | 2 pt | 5 cups |
| 150 ml | Double cream | ¼ pt | ½ cup |

'AS SURE AS GOD'S IN GLOUCESTERSHIRE' – this saying probably referred to the number of abbeys in the area. By 1535, with more than half the county in the hands of the church, it had ironic overtones!

THE MARKET SQUARE AT STOW (see page 24)

Radiating eight roads, Stow's market square forms the centre of the town's activity. The Medieval Cross, with its 19th century headstone, is a focal point, standing next to the town's stocks which visitors are invited to try for size!

1. Melt the butter in a pan, add the lobster shells, shallots and bay leaf. Fry gently for about 10 minutes without browning the shallots. Crush the shells very carefully and cook for a further 5 minutes.
2. Season with salt and pepper, then add the flour and tomato purée. Stir well until blended. Add the stock gradually and simmer for 5 minutes.
3. Strain the sauce and transfer to a liquidiser. Add the lobster meat and blend very gently.
4. Pour the sauce into a clean pan, add the cream and reheat, but do not boil. Pour a little sauce over each quenelle and serve the rest separately.


## SCALLOPS IN BACON                                     *Serves 5*

Lower Slaughter is a picturebook village and boasts an imposing manor house dating from 1600, now a lovely hotel. The chef recommends this stunningly simple but irresistible dish.

| Metric | | lb/oz | U.S.A. |
|---|---|---|---|
| | 5 Scallops, even sized, fresh or frozen | | |
| 1 | Garlic clove, crushed | 1 | 1 |
| 60 g | Butter | 2 oz | ¼ cup |
| ½ | Lemon, juice of | ½ | ½ |
| 5 | Rashers of bacon | 5 | 5 |
| 5 | Cocktail sticks | 5 | 5 |
| 30 g | Butter, for serving | 1 oz | 2 tbsp |
| 2 tbsp | Parsley, chopped | 2 tbsp | 2 tbsp |

1. To make the garlic butter, beat the crushed garlic into the butter until well mixed. Pass through a fine sieve.
2. Place in a lidded container and chill until required.
3. Season the scallops with salt, pepper and the lemon juice.
4. Remove the rind from the bacon and wrap a piece around each scallop. Secure with a cocktail stick.
5. Heat a heavy based pan and melt the garlic butter. Add the scallops and cook gently for about 5 minutes. If the bacon is not crispy by this time, place the scallops under the grill for a few minutes. Melt the butter.
6. Place the scallops on a heated serving dish, coat with the hot melted butter and sprinkle with chopped parsley.

*"Many's the long night I've dreamed of cheese
– toasted, mostly."*                         Treasure Island
ROBERT LOUIS STEVENSON, 1850-1894

## MUSSELS IN GARLIC AND CHEESE                         *Serves 8*

Shellfish aficionados will love this starter from the Rose Tree
Restaurant in Bourton-on-the-Water.

| Metric | | lb/oz | U.S.A. |
|---|---|---|---|
| 2.5 kg | Fresh mussels | 5 lb | 5 lb |
| 30 g | Butter | 1 oz | 2 tbsp |
| 1 | Small onion, chopped | 1 | ⅓ cup |
| 2 tbsp | White wine | 2 tbsp | 2 tbsp |
| 225 g | Cheddar cheese, grated | 8 oz | 2 cups |
| 225 g | Gruyère cheese, grated | 8 oz | 2 cups |
| | For the garlic butter: | | |
| 225 g | Butter | 8 oz | 1 cup |
| 10 | Garlic cloves, crushed | 10 | 10 |

1. Clean and beard the mussels, being careful to throw away
   any that are broken or open.
2. Melt the butter in a pan and gently fry the onion until
   transparent but not browned.
3. Add the white wine and when simmering add the mussels.
   Shake while simmering until the mussels are open and
   cooked. Discard any that do not open, then allow the
   mussels to cool.
4. To make the garlic butter, cream the butter with the
   crushed garlic and freshly ground black pepper.
5. Remove half of each mussel shell and fill the remaining half
   with the mussel and garlic butter. Arrange on individual
   heatproof dishes.
6. Mix the grated cheeses together and sprinkle over the
   mussels. Place under a pre-heated grill until the cheese is
   brown and bubbling, and serve immediately with French
   bread.

## SAUTE SCAMPI MORNAY                         *Serves 4-6*

Scampi are popular with young and old alike. In this recipe
from the Island House Restaurant, Chipping Campden, the
delicately spiced fish is coated in a creamy cheese sauce.

| Metric | | lb/oz | U.S.A. |
|---|---|---|---|
| 450 g | Scampi | 1 lb | 1 lb |
| 300 ml | Mornay sauce | ½ pt | 1 cup |
| 60 g | Margarine | 2 oz | ¼ cup |
| 1 | Mixed herbs, pinch of | 1 | 1 |
| 1 | Garlic clove, crushed | 1 | 1 |

1. Make the mornay sauce.
2. Melt the margarine in a pan. Add the herbs, garlic and scampi, and sauté for 1½ minutes. Add the mornay sauce, season with salt and pepper to taste, and cook for a further 2 minutes. Serve immediately, accompanied with French bread.

## Mornay sauce

| Metric | | lb/oz | U.S.A. |
|---|---|---|---|
| 300 ml | Béchamel sauce (see below) | ½ pt | 1 cup |
| 1 | Egg yolk | 1 | 1 |
| 1 tbsp | Parmesan cheese, grated | 1 tbsp | 1 tbsp |
| 1 tbsp | Cheddar or Gruyère cheese, grated | 1 tbsp | 1 tbsp |
| 2 tbsp | Double cream | 2 tbsp | 2 tbsp |
| 1 | Cayenne pepper, pinch of | 1 | 1 |
| 2 tbsp | Fish stock* | 2 tbsp | 2 tbsp |

1. Make the béchamel sauce as described below, but add the egg yolk before bringing the flavoured milk to the boil. Stir until the egg yolk is cooked.
2. Stir in the grated cheese and cream. Add the cayenne pepper and season with salt and pepper to taste.
3. Stir in the fish stock until you have the right consistency.

*Only add fish stock if the sauce is to be used for a fish dish. A little milk will thin the sauce if necessary.

## Béchamel sauce

| Metric | | lb/oz | U.S.A. |
|---|---|---|---|
| 300 ml | Milk | ½ pt | 1 cup |
| 1 | Small onion, chopped | 1 | ⅓ cup |
| 1 | Carrot, chopped | 1 | 1 |
| 1 | Stick of celery, chopped | 1 | 1 |
| 1 | Bay leaf | 1 | 1 |
| 1 | Clove | 1 | 1 |
| ½ tsp | Mace, ground | ½ tsp | ½ tsp |
| 2 | Peppercorns | 2 | 2 |
| 30 g | Butter | 1 oz | 2 tbsp |
| 45 g | Flour | 1½ oz | ¼ cup |

1. Place the milk and vegetables in a saucepan and bring slowly to the boil, then add the herbs and spices. Cover the pan with a tightly fitting lid.
2. Remove the saucepan from the heat and leave covered for half an hour to infuse.
3. Strain off the milk and remove the vegetables from the pan.
4. Melt the butter in the pan slowly, add the flour and cook for a few minutes, stirring all the time. Be careful not to brown the mixture.
5. Stir the flavoured milk gradually into the flour until the mixture is smooth. *For mornay sauce, see instructions above.* For use in other recipes, bring to the boil, stirring all the time.

## ROAST RACK OF ENGLISH LAMB WITH CUCUMBER AND FRESH MINT YOGURT

*Serves 4*

There is nothing more succulent than tender English lamb cooked until it is just pink and served with fresh young vegetables. Try it with the cucumber and fresh mint yogurt served in the Kings Arms Hotel at Chipping Campden.

| Metric | | lb/oz | U.S.A. |
|--------|--------------------------------|-------|--------|
| | 1 English best end of lamb | | |
| 30 g | Dripping | 1 oz | 2 tbsp |
| 1 | Rosemary sprig | 1 | 1 |
| 150 ml | Plain yogurt | ¼ pt | ½ cup |
| 1 | Bunch of fresh mint, chopped | 1 | 1 |
| 1 | Lemon, grated rind | 1 | 1 |
| ½ | Cucumber, thinly sliced | ½ | ½ |
| 4 | Fresh mint sprigs | 4 | 4 |

1. Set the oven to 180°C, 350°F, Gas Mark 4.
2. Melt the dripping in a roasting pan and add the lamb and rosemary. Roast for 20 minutes or till the meat is pink.
3. Season the yogurt with salt and freshly ground black pepper. Add the chopped mint and lemon rind to taste.
4. Remove the lamb from the oven and carve. Place on a warm serving dish, and garnish with the cucumber. Pour over the yogurt and decorate with mint sprigs.

*"Lane: There were no cucumbers in the market this morning, Sir. I went down twice.*
*Algernon: No cucumbers!*
*Lane: No Sir, not even for ready money."*
*The Importance of Being Earnest*
*OSCAR WILDE, 1854-1900*

# BROCHETTES BENJAMIN                    *Serves 4*

This is a speciality of the Chef at the Old Manse Hotel in Bourton-on-the-Water. He threads kebab skewers with lamb, (150 g, 5 oz per head), bay leaves, bacon, green or red peppers, button mushrooms and onions. Next, he marinates them overnight in a pint of red wine and a quarter of a pint of olive oil laced with brandy and flavoured with parsley stalks, mixed herbs, salt, pepper and diced vegetables. The kebabs are served on a savoury rice containing bacon, onion, mushrooms, peppers and peas, and topped with this delicious sauce:

| Metric | | lb/oz | U.S.A. |
|---|---|---|---|
| 3 tbsp | Vinegar | 3 tbsp | ¼ cup |
| 6 | Peppercorns, crushed | 6 | 6 |
| 3 | Egg yolks | 3 | 3 |
| 225 g | Butter, melted | ½ lb | 1 cup |
| ½ | Lemon, juice of | ½ | ½ |
| 1 | Cayenne pepper, pinch of | 1 | 1 |
| 2 | Garlic cloves, crushed | 2 | 2 |
| 150 ml | Double cream | ¼ pt | ½ cup |

1. Put the vinegar into a small pan with the peppercorns and bring to the boil. Boil for a few minutes until the vinegar has reduced in quantity by half. Allow to cool and add 2 tbsp of water.
2. Transfer the mixture to a bowl and whisk in the egg yolks over a pan of hot water until the mixture is creamy.
3. Continue whisking and add the melted butter, a little at a time. Add the lemon juice, cayenne pepper and a pinch of salt. Beat well.
4. Strain through muslin and add the garlic to the sauce. Whip the cream and fold into the sauce. Keep warm.
5. **To make savoury rice,** place the rice in a pan of boiling water, add a pinch of salt and bring the water back to the boil. Lower the heat and simmer for 15-20 minutes until cooked.
6. While the rice is cooking, place the brochettes under a hot grill and cook, turning occasionally.
7. Heat the oil in a large pan and gently fry the bacon, onions and mushrooms, then stir in the rest of the ingredients for the rice and cook for a few minutes.
8. When the rice is cooked, drain, and refresh with boiling water. Drain well then add to the pan with the bacon mixture and stir until hot.
9. Turn on to a warm serving dish, place the brochettes on top and coat with sauce.

*"The mountain sheep are sweeter,*
*But the valley sheep are fatter;*
*We therefore deemed it meeter*          The Misfortunes of Elphin
*To carry off the latter."*              T.L. PEACOCK, 1785-1866

# LAMB PORTFOLIO

*Serves 6*

These delicious pastry parcels are perfect for a dinner party. They are easy to dish, and can be prepared well ahead of time. Serve them with sauce, gravy, or just as they are. This recipe, and the one on page 37, come from the Old New Inn, Bourton-on-the-Water.

| *Metric* | | *lb/oz* | *U.S.A* |
|---|---|---|---|
| | *12 Lamb cutlets* | | |
| 60 g | *Butter* | 2 oz | ¼ cup |
| 1 | *Onion, peeled and diced* | 1 | ½ cup |
| 125 g | *Button mushrooms, diced* | 4 oz | 1 cup |
| 125 g | *Ham, diced* | 4 oz | 1 cup |
| 1 tbsp | *White wine* | 1 tbsp | 1 tbsp |
| 1 tbsp | *Tomato purée* | 1 tbsp | 1 tbsp |
| 450 g | *Flaky pastry* | 1 lb | 1 lb |
| 1 | *Egg, beaten* | 1 | 1 |

1. Set the oven to 200°C, 400°F, Gas Mark 6, and heat grill.
2. Grill the lamb cutlets until brown on one side. Allow to cool then take the meat off the bone.
3. Melt the butter in a pan, add the onions and cook until soft and transparent. Add the mushrooms and stir over a low heat.
4. Add the ham, stir in the wine and tomato purée, and season well with salt and pepper. Cook for a minute longer then allow to cool.
5. Roll out the pastry and cut out six 7-10 cm (3-4") squares (the size will depend on the size of your cutlets).
6. Place the meat from two cutlets in the middle of each square and top the meat with the onion mixture.
7. Coat the pastry edges with egg then gather the corners to the middle and press together to make a pyramid.
8. Place on a baking tray and brush the outside of the pastry with the remaining egg. Bake for 15-20 minutes until golden brown.

## CHIPPING NORTON

The 13th century market first brought prosperity to the town through the flourishing wool trade. Today the large Victorian mill in the valley still produces tweed and maintains Chipping Norton's reputation as a cloth making town.

The 19th century Town Hall stands in the Chepynge (which is medieval for market place) alongside hotels, inns and shops which date from the 17th, 18th and 19th centuries.

A picturesque row of 17th century almshouses lies close to the town's Perpendicular style church which, restored by overzealous Victorians, consequently lacks an atmosphere of antiquity. However, it has retained its unusual porch with vaulted ceiling and has a carved sheep's head to greet all who enter!

# LAMB KEBABS MARINADED IN
# CORIANDER AND GARLIC

*Serves 4*

A good recipe for summer barbecues from the Gallery Restaurant, Broadway.

| Metric | | lb/oz | U.S.A. |
|---|---|---|---|
| 500 g | Lamb (taken from the leg, trimmed and cut into 2.5 cm, 1" cubes) | 1 lb | 1 lb |
| 3 tbsp | Oil | 3 tbsp | ¼ cup |
| 1 tbsp | Lemon juice | 1 tbsp | 1 tbsp |
| 2 | Garlic cloves, crushed | 2 | 2 |
| 1 tbsp | Whole coriander, crushed | 1 tbsp | 1 tbsp |
| 8 | Button mushrooms | 8 | 8 |
| 2 | Small onions, peeled and quartered | 2 | 2 |
| 1 | Green pepper, de-seeded and cut into chunks | 1 | 1 |
| 8 | Small firm tomatoes | 8 | 8 |

1. Marinade the lamb cubes in the oil, lemon juice, garlic, coriander and seasoning for at least two hours but preferably 4-6 hours.
2. Thread 8 skewers with an equal mixture of lamb cubes, mushrooms, onion quarters, green pepper and tomatoes.
3. Strain the marinade, discard the coriander and garlic pieces and brush the kebabs with the remaining mixture.
4. Cook under a low grill for 10-15 minutes turning every 5 minutes and brushing with the marinade.
5. Serve on plain boiled rice with a green salad.

*"Then will he look as fierce as a Cotswold lion".*
NICHOLAS UDALL

THE COTSWOLD LION is alive and well, but don't be alarmed — it is not as fierce as it sounds, just an ancient breed of sheep! They are on view at the Rare Breeds Trust at Cotswold Farm Park.

## OLD NEW INN LAMBS' KIDNEYS IN PEPPER AND CREAM SAUCE
*Serves 8*

Colourful peppers combine with cream and wine to make an exotic dish out of the common kidney.

| Metric | | lb/oz | U.S.A. |
|---|---|---|---|
| 1.75 kg | Lambs' kidneys | 4 lb | 4 lb |
| 125 g | Plain flour | 4 oz | 1 cup |
| 2 | Peppers, green or red | 2 | 2 |
| 2 | Onions, large | 2 | 2 |
| 225 g | Butter | 8 oz | 1 cup |
| 125 ml | Medium white wine (optional) | 4 fl oz | ½ cup |
| 300 ml | Whipping cream | ½ pt | 1 cup |

1. Set the oven to 180°C, 350°F, Gas Mark 4.
2. Skin and core the kidneys, then toss in the flour, reserving 1 tbsp.
3. Slice onions into rings and de-seed and slice peppers.
4. Melt a third of the butter in a frying pan and when it begins to froth put in the kidneys.* Brown them on both sides then remove and place in an ovenproof dish.
5. Put the onions and peppers together in the pan with a little more butter and fry gently until the onions are transparent but not browned. Remove with a draining spoon and arrange on top of the kidneys.
6. Heat the wine in a small saucepan until boiling then simmer until reduced by half.
7. Melt the remaining butter in the frying pan and add the reserved flour and stir until you have a roux. Stir in the cream and wine and cook gently until thickened.
8. Season well with salt and pepper then pour over the kidneys. Place in the oven and cook for ¾ hour.

* A little oil with the butter helps to stop it burning — Editor.

*"There are black sheep in every flock."* 19th Century proverb

BROADWAY HILL

A large bonfire was once lit on the summit of the Hill by a curious Lady Coventry who wished to know if it could be seen from her home near Worcester. Discovering that it was visible, she persuaded her husband to build a tower to mark the site of the beacon. Both Broadway Hill and its tower are now a central feature of 'Country Park'.

## AGNINAM EXCALDATAM ET CONCHICHLAM
## DE PISA SIMPLICI
## HOT LAMB STEW WITH BAKED PEAS                    *Serves 4*

Coriander, lovage and cumin combine to add an exotic flavour
to this dish from the Kings Hotel, Cirencester.

| Metric | | lb/oz | U.S.A. |
|---|---|---|---|
| 750 g | Lamb | 1½ lb | 1½ lb |
| 2 | Onions, finely chopped | 2 | 1 cup |
| | Whole black peppercorns | | |
| ¾ tsp | Coriander | ¾ tsp | ¾ tsp |
| ¾ tsp | Lovage | ¾ tsp | ¾ tsp |
| ¾ tsp | Cumin | ¾ tsp | ¾ tsp |
| 1 tbsp | Liquamen* | 1 tbsp | 1 tbsp |
| 3 tbsp | Oil | 3 tbsp | ¼ cup |
| 125 ml | Red wine | 4 fl oz | ½ cup |
| 1 tbsp | Cornflour | 1 tbsp | 1 tbsp |

1. Prepare and start cooking the peas as described below.
2. Cut the lamb into small pieces and place in a casserole dish.
   Sprinkle over the onion.
3. Place the peppercorns, coriander, lovage, cumin,
   liquamen, oil and wine in a mortar and pound until you
   have a sauce.
4. Pour the sauce over the meat. After the peas have cooked
   for 1¼ hours, turn the oven up to 180°C, 350°F, Gas Mark
   4 and place them in the bottom of the oven. Put the
   casserole in the middle and cook until the meat is tender.
5. Slake the cornflour with a little water in a small bowl and
   stir into the casserole to thicken the juices.
6. Serve immediately with the Conchicla of plain peas.

**Conchicla of plain peas**

| Metric | | lb/oz | U.S.A |
|---|---|---|---|
| 250 g | Dried peas** | 8 oz | ½ lb |
| 1 | Bouquet garni | 1 | 1 |
| | Whole black peppercorns | | |
| ½ tsp | Lovage | ½ tsp | ½ tsp |
| ½ tsp | Oregano | ½ tsp | ½ tsp |
| | Liquamen, to taste* | | |
| 125 ml | Wine | 4 fl oz | ½ cup |
| 2 tbsp | Oil | 2 tbsp | 2 tbsp |

*Liquamen was a fermented fish stock — use 2 tbsp Tamara
mixed with ¾ pt of stock made with a few drops of anchovy
essence. This is the nearest thing one can find these days.*

**1 can (15 oz) peas may be substituted. Add herbs and
flavourings and bake on the bottom shelf for the last 20
minutes of the lamb's cooking time.*

1. The peas must be soaked for 24 hours prior to cooking.
   Place the peas in a pan and cover with water. Bring to the
   boil and skim off the froth.
2. Cook gently for a few minutes while you crush the
   peppercorns, lovage and oregano together. Moisten this
   with the liquamen, wine and oil to make a sauce.
3. Place peas and bouquet garni in an earthenware dish,
   cover with sauce and bake at 150°C, 300°F, Gas Mark 2,
   for 1¼ hours, then follow the instructions above.

## ENTRECOTE RUSSIAN                                    *Serves 4*

Vodka and soured cream add an eastern European flavour to
this dish from the Royalist Hotel, Stow-on-the-Wold.

| Metric | | lb/oz | U.S.A. |
|---|---|---|---|
| | 4 Sirloin steaks | | |
| 30 g | Butter | 1 oz | 2 tbsp |
| 2 | Onions, chopped | 2 | 1 cup |
| 1 | Green pepper, chopped | 1 | ½ cup |
| 250 g | Mushrooms, chopped | 8 oz | 2 cups |
| 2 tbsp | Vodka | 2 tbsp | 2 tbsp |
| 1 tsp | Mixed herbs | 1 tsp | 1 tsp |
| 150 ml | Soured cream | ¼ pt | ½ cup |
| 1 tsp | Sugar | 1 tsp | 1 tsp |

1. Melt the butter in a large pan and sauté the onions until
   transparent but not browned.
2. Add the pepper and mushrooms and cook gently for a few
   minutes.
3. Put in the steaks and cook for a few minutes on each side.
   Season with a pinch of salt and some freshly ground black
   pepper, then pour over the vodka and flambé.
4. Stir in the mixed herbs, soured cream and sugar, and serve
   immediately.

*"The winter evening settles down*                          Preludes
*With smell of steaks in passage ways."* T.S. ELIOT, 1888-1965

### BROADWAY TOWER

Built in 1800, this Gothic folly was
created by the Earl of Coventry to
satisfy his wife's whim. Stand on
the tower's castellated roof on a
clear day and you will see
spectacular views that stretch over
fourteen different counties.

WILLIAM MORRIS and his pre-
Raphaelite friends once spent a
few weeks lodging in Broadway
Tower. However, their enjoyment
was marred by the fact that they
had to carry their own food all the
way up from the town!

## BROADWAY

Headquarters of both Oliver Cromwell and Charles I at different times during the Civil War, the picturesque Lygon Arms was also a favourite holiday spot with the 19th century pre-Raphaelite artists William Morris, Rossetti and Burne-Jones. Today Broadway's elegant Elizabethan and Georgian houses, still standing before broad greens, convey the unchanging atmosphere of sedate 18th century village life.

# PORK BRION
*Serves 4*

An unusual dish which comes to the table topped with bubbling hot cheese. The recipe is the creation of Mr. B.J. Tanner, proprietor/chef of the Warren Olde Worlde Restaurant, Bourton-on-the-Water.

| Metric | | lb/oz | U.S.A |
|--------|--------------------------|--------|--------|
| 1 kg | 1 Loin of pork* | 2 lb | 2 lb |
| 300 ml | Cheese sauce | ½ pt | 1 cup |
| 300 ml | Dry cider | ½ pt | 1 cup |
| 3 tbsp | Almonds, flaked | 3 tbsp | ¼ cup |
| 4 | Pineapple rings | 4 | 4 |
| 125 g | Stilton cheese, sliced | 4 oz | ¼ lb |
| 4 tbsp | Cheddar cheese, grated | 4 tbsp | ⅓ cup |
| 1 tsp | Mixed herbs | 1 tsp | 1 tsp |

1. Heat the grill. Remove any bones from the pork and cut into four pieces. Grill until cooked, turning once.
2. Make the cheese sauce. Heat the cider to boiling point.
3. Place the pork in an ovenproof serving dish, pour over the cider to come halfway up the pork pieces and sprinkle with the almonds.
4. Place the pineapple rings and sliced stilton on the almonds. Pour over the cheese sauce.
5. Mix the grated cheese and herbs together. Sprinkle over the top, and brown under a hot grill. Serve immediately.

*\* Equivalent to 4 large chops — Editor*

## Cheese sauce

| Metric | | lb/oz | U.S.A. |
|--------|--------------------------|--------|--------|
| 20 g | Butter | ¾ oz | 1 tbsp |
| 2 tbsp | Plain flour | 2 tbsp | 2 tbsp |
| 300 ml | Milk | ½ pt | 1 cup |
| 60 g | Cheddar and Parmesan cheese, grated | 2 oz | ½ cup |
| 1 | Dry mustard, pinch of | 1 | 1 |
| 1 | Cayenne pepper, pinch of | 1 | 1 |

1. Melt the butter in a pan. Add the flour and blend to make a smooth roux. Cook for 2-3 minutes, stirring continuously.
2. Add the milk gradually, stirring all the time. Bring to the boil and cook for 1-2 minutes, still stirring. Season with salt and pepper to taste.
3. Remove from the heat and stir in the cheese, mustard and cayenne pepper. Stir until the cheese has melted.

## ARLINGTON ROW, BIBURY

Originally a 14th century wool store which grew into a 17th century weaving factory, this famous row of cottages faces Arlington Mill across Rack Meadow. The Mill was built on the site of an earlier one that was recorded in the Doomsday book.

## FILLETS OF PORK CHARLOTTE                          *Serves 2*

This delicately flavoured dish from the Broadway Hotel can be reproduced in less than half an hour if you have assembled all the ingredients beforehand.

| Metric | | lb/oz | U.S.A. |
|--------|--------------------------------|--------|--------|
| | 2×175g (6oz) Pork tenderloin | | |
| 2 tbsp | Flour | 2 tbsp | ¼ cup |
| 60 g | Butter | 2 oz | ¼ cup |
| 4 | Shallots, chopped | 4 | 1 cup |
| 8 | Button mushrooms | 8 | 8 |
| 1 tbsp | Brandy | 1 tbsp | 1 tbsp |
| 150 ml | Double cream | ¼ pt | ½ cup |
| 2 | Tomatoes | 2 | 2 |
| 30 g | Prawns, peeled | 1 oz | ¼ cup |

1. Slice the pork into 1 cm (½") rounds and coat with flour seasoned with salt and pepper.
2. Melt the butter in a large pan and add the shallots. Cook gently until transparent but not browned.
3. Add the mushrooms and pork. Cook gently, turning the pork occasionally, for 10 minutes or until it is cooked.
4. Pour over the brandy and flambé.
5. Add the double cream and cook until the sauce is reduced in quantity and thickened. Do not boil.
6. Quarter and de-seed the tomatoes. Add to the sauce and allow to heat through. Finally, add the prawns.
7. Serve the pork on rice or noodles, topped with the sauce.

## GLOUCESTERSHIRE ESCALOPES OF PORK WITH APRICOTS                          *Serves 4*

A rich and colourful dish from the Swan Hotel, Bibury.

| Metric | | lb/oz | U.S.A. |
|--------|----------------------------------------------|--------|---------|
| | 2× 500 g (1 lb) Pork fillets | | |
| 125 g | Double Gloucester cheese, cut into four slices | 4 oz | ¼ lb |
| 4 | Apricots, halved, stoned and skinned | 4 | 4 |
| 125 g | Butter | 4 oz | ½ cup |
| 2 | Brandy measures | 2 | 2 |
| 600 ml | Whipping cream | 1 pt | 2½ cups |
| 1 tsp | Paprika | 1 tsp | 1 tsp |

1. Trim the pork fillets and cut each in half to make four slices. Using a wooden rolling pin, flatten into escalopes.
2. Lay the escalopes flat and season with salt and pepper. Place a slice of cheese on one half of each escalope. Press two apricot halves very lightly on top of each slice of cheese and fold the pork over.

3. Melt the butter in a large pan, place the pork escalopes in the pan and cook very gently for about 10 minutes, turning four or five times. Remove and keep warm.
4. Drain any remaining butter from the pan and return the pork escalopes to the pan. Pour over the brandy and ignite. Add the cream and stir until it thickens.
5. Transfer to a warm serving dish, sprinkle with paprika and serve immediately.

## BARBECUED SPARE RIBS                                   *Serves 3-4*

An inexpensive and popular supper dish from the Fosse Manor Hotel near Stow-on-the-Wold.

| Metric | | lb/oz | U.S.A. |
|---|---|---|---|
| 1 kg | Pork spare ribs | 2 lb | 2 lb |
| 2-3 | Red colouring, drops of | 2-3 | 2-3 |
| 1 | Ginger, pinch of | 1 | 1 |
| 1 | Cinnamon, pinch of | 1 | 1 |
| 2 | Garlic cloves, crushed | 2 | 2 |
| | Aniseed cordial, to taste | | |
| 30 g | Butter | 1 oz | 2 tbsp |
| 30 g | Flour | 1 oz | ¼ cup |

1. Cut the spare ribs into pieces, about two bones to every piece.
2. Place in a saucepan, add the colouring, ginger, cinnamon, cloves and aniseed cordial, and enough water to cover. Boil gently until tender then drain off liquor and reserve.
3. Melt the butter in another saucepan. Stir in the flour and cook for 1-2 minutes, stirring continuously.
4. Add the liquor carefully, blending it into the roux. Bring to the boil and simmer for 2-3 minutes.
5. To serve, pour the barbecue sauce over the spare ribs.

### CIRENCESTER (overleaf)

Cirencester stands on the site of Corinium, Roman Britain's second largest city. In Roman times the Fosse Way, Ermin Street and Akeman Street all met here, but only the amphitheatre remains above ground today. Fine Roman remains may be seen in the Corinium museum. Still a busy market town, Cirencester market was mentioned in the Doomsday Book and is still held every week.

The accepted source of the River Thames is at nearby Thames Head.

Cirencester was one of Britain's first conference centres. It was chosen by King Canute as the venue for an assembly in 1020 and became a popular place for holding important meetings.

| | |
|---|---|
| A FRAGMENT OF PLASTER discovered in 1868 on a New Road site has been variously thought to be a word square reading: 'Arepo the sower guides the wheels at work', or a secret Christian symbol based on the word 'Paternoster'. | ROTAS OPERA TENET AREPO SATOR |

CIRENCESTER PARISH CHURCH

Standing at 134 ft, the Perpendicular tower is an impressive reminder of the town's immense wealth during the 14th and 15th century. Inside is a figure of a boy which was used as a reminder for alms-giving to charity schools — an early forerunner of the high street collecting boxes. The church porch at one time served as the town hall.

Goblets Wine Bar in Broadway is owned by the Lygon Arms. The chef uses local home-made bangers in the dish below, but the sauce will add a sparkle to everyday sausages, too. Minna's chicken, which follows, is another of his creations.

## MILD MUSTARD SAUSAGES                               Serves 4

| Metric | | lb/oz | U.S.A |
|---|---|---|---|
| 1 kg | Sausages | 2 lb | 2 lb |
| | Oil for frying | | |
| 250 g | Onions, chopped | 8 oz | 2 cups |
| 250 g | Mushrooms, chopped | 8 oz | 2 cups |
| 300 ml | Béchamel sauce (see p.31) | ½ pt | 1 cup |
| 2 tbsp | Dijon mustard | 2 tbsp | 2 tbsp |

1. Make the béchamel sauce and stir in the Dijon mustard. Mix together well and keep warm.
2. Place the sausages under a hot grill and cook gently, turning occasionally.
3. Put a little oil in a pan and fry the onions gently until transparent but not browned.
4. Add the mushrooms and cook for a few more minutes.
5. Transfer to a warm dish and pour the sauce over.

## MINNA'S CHICKEN                                      Serves 6

| Metric | | lb/oz | U.S.A. |
|---|---|---|---|
| 1.25 kg | Cooked, boned chicken meat | 2½ lb | 2½ lb |
| 2-3 tbsp | Salad cream | 2-3 tbsp | ¼ cup |
| 500 ml | Two cans of condensed chicken soup | 16 oz | 16 oz |
| 400 ml | Evaporated milk | 14 oz | 14 oz |
| 60 g | Cheddar cheese, grated | 2 oz | ½ cup |
| 2-3 tsp | Curry powder | 2-3 tsp | 3 tsp |
| 250 g | Broccoli, cooked | 8 oz | ½ lb |

1. Cut the meat into small pieces. Light the oven.
2. Place the salad cream, soup, milk, cheese and curry powder in a pan and heat gently, stirring all the time.
3. Layer the chicken and broccoli in an ovenproof dish, pour over the sauce and heat through in a moderately hot oven.
4. Serve on a bed of rice accompanied with broccoli.

## BURY BARN CHICKEN                                    *Serves 4*

On the roundabout outside Burford, a large medieval barn has
been converted into a restaurant and banqueting hall. This
recipe for their popular chicken dish is easy to follow.

| Metric | | lb/oz | U.S.A |
|---|---|---|---|
| | 4 Chicken breasts | | |
| 2 tbsp | White wine | 2 tbsp | 2 tbsp |
| 250 g | Mushrooms, sliced | 8 oz | 2½ cups |
| 1 | Garlic clove, crushed | 1 | 1 |
| 60 g | Butter | 2 oz | ¼ cup |

1. Cut each breast of chicken horizontally to make a pocket in
   which to stuff the filling.
2. Put the white wine in a pan and add the mushrooms and
   garlic. Cook gently until the liquid is absorbed and the
   mushrooms are soft. Press them into the chicken breasts.
3. Melt the butter in a pan and gently fry the chicken breasts
   for a few minutes on each side until cooked.

*"I want there to be no peasant in my kingdom so poor
that he cannot have a chicken in his pot every Sunday."*
                          (Attr.) HENRY IV, of France, 1553-1610

## SPICED BREAST OF CHICKEN                           *Serves 4*

Curry powder and cayenne combine with lemon juice to add a
spicy touch to this creamy chicken creation from the Swan
Hotel, Bibury.

| Metric | | lb/oz | U.S.A. |
|---|---|---|---|
| | 4 Chicken breasts | | |
| 60 g | Butter | 2 oz | ¼ cup |
| 1 tsp | Curry powder | 1 tsp | 1 tsp |
| 175 g | Mushrooms, sliced | 6 oz | 2 cups |
| 1 | Cayenne pepper, pinch of | 1 | 1 |
| ½ | Lemon, juice of | ½ | ½ |
| 150 ml | Whipping cream | ¼ pt | ½ cup |
| 3 tbsp | Parsley, chopped | 3 tbsp | ¼ cup |

1. Set the oven to 180°C, 350°F, Gas Mark 4.
2. Melt the butter in a pan, add the chicken breasts, and cook
   gently for about 12 minutes, turning once.
3. Add the curry powder and cook for a further 4-5 minutes,
   stirring well.
4. Add the mushrooms and cook for a few minutes, then add
   the cayenne pepper, lemon juice and cream.
5. Place in a casserole, cover and cook in a moderate oven for
   about 45 minutes.
6. Garnish with the parsley and serve immediately.

## POLO AT CIRENCESTER PARK

Completed early in the 18th century, Cirencester Park has about 3,000 acres of grounds. The Park, once popular with the poet Alexander Pope, today attracts polo enthusiasts including the Prince of Wales. During the summer, matches take place every Sunday.

## BREAST OF CHICKEN STUFFED WITH PRAWNS AND SMOKED SALMON
*Serves 2*

Chef Smart of the Fosse Manor Hotel on the Fosseway near Stow-on-the-Wold has contributed this unusual and luxurious variation on Chicken Kiev.

| Metric | | lb/oz | U.S.A. |
|---|---|---|---|
| | 2 Chicken breasts | | |
| 60 g | Prawns, shelled and chopped | 2 oz | ½ cup |
| 60 g | Smoked salmon, chopped | 2 oz | ½ cup |
| 2 | Parsley sprigs, chopped | 2 | 2 |
| 125 g | Butter, softened | 4 oz | ½ cup |
| 2 tbsp | Flour | 2 tbsp | 2 tbsp |
| 1 | Egg, beaten | 1 | 1 |
| 4 tbsp | Fresh breadcrumbs | 4 tbsp | ⅓ cup |
| | Oil for frying | | |

1. Mix the prawns, salmon and parsley into the butter.
2. Flatten out the chicken breasts using the back of a wooden spoon.
3. Place half the fish butter in the centre of each breast. Fold the left edge over the butter, then overlap the right side, making a conical-shaped parcel.
4. Dust the chicken with flour, coat with egg and roll in breadcrumbs.
5. Fry in deep fat for 8-10 minutes and serve immediately.

## STOW FAIR

Stow Fair is held in May and October and is renowned throughout Europe. Once the biggest livestock market in Britain, the largest trade today is in horses and farm equipment.

## PHEASANT IN PORT WINE
## WITH SAVOURY DUMPLINGS

*Serves 2*

This rich and succulent dish from the Broadway Hotel would no doubt have been popular with the Abbots of Pershore, who inhabited the premises in the sixteenth century. The architecture combines Vale of Evesham half timbers with mellow Cotswold stone.

| Metric | | lb/oz | U.S.A. |
|---|---|---|---|
| | 1 Pheasant (oven ready) | | |
| 300 ml | Brown game sauce | ½ pt | 1 cup |
| 4 | Savoury suet dumplings | 4 | 4 |
| 2 tbsp | Seasoned flour | 2 tbsp | 2 tbsp |
| 60 g | Butter | 2 oz | ¼ cup |
| 1 | Onion, chopped | 1 | ½ cup |
| 3 tbsp | Port | 3 tbsp | ¼ cup |
| 6 | Button onions | 6 | 6 |
| 6 | Button mushrooms | 6 | 6 |

1. Set the oven to 180°C, 350°F, Gas Mark 4. Make the sauce and dumplings.
2. Cut the pheasant in half and coat with flour seasoned with salt and pepper. Melt half the butter in a pan and fry the pheasant with the chopped onion until lightly browned.
3. Pour over the port and flambé. Simmer, uncovered, for 5-10 minutes, add the brown sauce and stir lightly.
4. In a separate pan, melt the remaining butter and fry the button onions and mushrooms until browned. When the bird is three parts cooked, add the onions and mushrooms.
5. Transfer the contents to a casserole and arrange the dumplings on the top. Cover and place in the oven until cooked (about 1 hour). Check the liquid level occasionally and top up with boiling water if necessary.

### Brown game sauce

| Metric | | lb/oz | U.S.A. |
|---|---|---|---|
| 15 g | Dripping | ½ oz | 1 tbsp |
| 1 | Small carrot, chopped | 1 | 1 |
| 1 | Small onion, chopped | 1 | 1 |
| 30 g | Mushroom stalks, chopped | 1 oz | ¼ cup |
| 15 g | Flour | ½ oz | 1 tbsp |
| 300 ml | Stock | ½ pt | 1 cup |
| 2 tbsp | Juices from roast game, if available | 2 tbsp | 2 tbsp |

1. Melt the dripping in a large pan and add the carrot and onion. Fry slowly until golden brown.
2. Add the mushroom stalks and fry for a few minutes.
3. Stir in flour. Fry very gently till cooked and golden brown.
4. Gradually stir in the stock. Bring almost to boiling point, then reduce the heat and add the game juices.
5. Season with salt and pepper to taste and simmer gently for half an hour. Strain before serving.

## Savoury suet dumplings

*Makes about 8*

| Metric | | lb/oz | U.S.A. |
|---|---|---|---|
| 225 g | Flour | 8 oz | 2 cups |
| ½ tsp | Baking powder | ½ tsp | ½ tsp |
| 60 g | Shredded suet | 2 oz | ½ cup |
| 1 | Mixed herbs, pinch of | 1 | 1 |

1. Sift the flour into a bowl with the baking powder and a pinch of salt. Stir in the suet and mixed herbs and mix to a firm dough with a little cold water.
2. Form into small balls and place on top of the casserole for about an hour (or drop into boiling stock for 3 minutes then reduce the heat and simmer for about 25 minutes) until the dumplings are soft and fluffy.

---

## MALMESBURY PHEASANT WITH APPLES

*Serves 2*

---

*"Where the apple reddens*
*Never pry —*
*Lest we lose our Edens,*
*Eve and I."*

A Woman's Last Word
ROBERT BROWNING, 1812-1889

---

The Lords of the Manor Hotel at Upper Slaughter uses a local apple wine in this recipe. Vintage cider may be substituted if apple wine is not available.

| Metric | | lb/oz | U.S.A. |
|---|---|---|---|
| | 1 Pheasant (oven ready) | | |
| 60 g | Butter | 2 oz | ¼ cup |
| 1 | Large onion, chopped | 1 | 1 cup |
| 350 g | Cooking apples, sliced | 12 oz | 3 cups |
| 150 ml | Malmesbury apple wine | ¼ pt | ½ cup |
| 150 ml | Whipping cream | ¼ pt | ½ cup |

1. Set the oven to 200°C, 400°F, Gas Mark 6.
2. Melt the butter in an ovenproof casserole and sauté the onion until tender.
3. Add the pheasant and brown on all sides to seal the meat.
4. Place the apple slices on top of the pheasant and season to taste with salt and pepper.
5. Pour over the wine, cover with tin foil or a tightly fitting casserole lid, and cook in the oven for 1½ hours or until the pheasant is tender.
6. Remove the casserole from the oven and stir in the cream just before serving to thicken the sauce.

THE LORDS OF THE MANOR Hotel and Restaurant is a 17th century manor house furnished with antiques and family pictures. It is still managed by the family whose home it has been for 200 years.

## ROAST PARTRIDGE PAPON WITH SPICED RED CABBAGE AND RED WINE SAUCE

*Serves 4*

The Centurion Rooms in Cirencester find partridge is popular when in season, and have supplied this recipe.

| Metric | | lb/oz | U.S.A. |
|---|---|---|---|
| | 4 Partridges | | |
| 30 g | Butter | 1 oz | 2 tbsp |
| 500 g | Red cabbage, finely chopped | 1 lb | 1 lb |
| 250 g | Cooking apples, chopped | 8 oz | 1½ cups |
| 1 tsp | Mixed spice | 1 tsp | 1 tsp |
| 1 | Garlic clove, crushed | 1 | 1 |
| 1 tbsp | Demerara sugar | 1 tbsp | 1 tbsp |
| 125 g | Onion, chopped | 4 oz | 1 cup |
| 150 ml | Red wine | ¼ pt | ½ cup |
| 30 g | Dripping | 1 oz | 2 tbsp |
| 1 tbsp | Cornflour | 1 tbsp | 1 tbsp |
| 2 tbsp | Parsley, chopped | 2 tbsp | 2 tbsp |

1. Set the oven to 170°C, 325°F, Gas Mark 3.
2. Melt the butter in an ovenproof casserole, and add the cabbage, apples, spice, garlic, sugar and onion. Pour over the red wine and stir well. Braise for 2½ hours.
3. Place the partridges in a baking pan with the dripping for the last hour of cooking.
4. Remove the birds. Strain off the liquor into a small saucepan. Place the cabbage mixture on a warm serving dish and arrange the birds on top.
5. Bring the liquor to the boil, adding a little more red wine or water if necessary. Slake the cornflour with a little cold water, then stir in to thicken.
6. Coat the partridges with the sauce and sprinkle with parsley.

## VENISON WITH BLOOD ORANGES    *Serves 4-5*

The Lygon Arms at Broadway is world famous. Here's how they like to serve their saddle of venison.

| Metric | | lb/oz | U.S.A. |
|---|---|---|---|
| | 1 Small saddle of venison | | |
| | 1 Small saddle of hare | | |
| 2 tsp | Mixed herbs | 2 tsp | 2 tsp |
| 125 g | Fresh breadcrumbs | 4 oz | 2 cups |
| 1 | Egg, beaten | 1 | 1 |
| 60 g | Dripping | 2 oz | ¼ cup |
| 300 ml | Good stock (veal if | ½ pt | 1 cup |
| | available) | | |
| 2 | Blood oranges, juice of | 2 | 2 |
| 225 g | Butter | 8 oz | 1 cup |
| | Croûtons | | |

1. Set the oven to 180°C, 350°F, Gas Mark 4.
2. Remove the meat from the bones of the hare and mince. Mix with the herbs and the breadcrumbs, and use enough egg to bind the mixture to a paste without making it wet.
3. Place in a well greased ovenproof dish and cook in the oven for 20 minutes.
4. Melt the dripping in a roasting pan and roast the venison for 20 minutes per 500 g (1 lb) or until pink.
5. Remove the venison and cut the meat off the bone. Dice the venison and press it back on the saddle bone alternating with wedges of hare forcemeat*. Place on a serving dish and keep warm.
6. To make the gravy, add the stock to the juices remaining in the roasting pan and bring to the boil.
7. Boil the orange juice in a small pan until reduced by half.
8. Reduce the heat and gradually whisk in the butter, piece by piece, until the mixture is thick.
9. Serve the meat and offer the blood orange butter and croûtons separately.

*Arrange neatly on a serving dish, if preferred – Editor.*

VENISON should always be hung well – for about 14 days before cooking. If it has not been hung, make a mixture of ground ginger and black pepper and rub all over the meat to preserve it. Check each day, adding more of the mixture if necessary. Wash off before cooking and dry the meat well.

MORE THAN THIRTY COACHES A DAY thundered through 18th century Burford, many passengers stopping for Burford 'bait' – the enormous meals provided for travellers, which often included venison poached from the nearby Wychwood forest.

SIMON WISDOM'S HOUSE (opposite) According to the plaque benefactor Simon Wisdom was the 'First Founder Of The Schole in Burford'. Established in 1571, the Grammar School for Boys was initially housed in this building.

## CUTLET OF VENISON, FLAMED WITH WHISKY, COOKED IN GAME SAUCE AND CREAM  *Serves 4*

The strong flavours of venison and whisky complement one another in this rich recipe from the Swan Hotel, Bibury.

| Metric | | lb/oz | U.S.A. |
|---|---|---|---|
| | 4 Venison cutlets | | |
| 600 ml | Game sauce | 1 pt | 2 cups |
| 125 g | Butter | 4 oz | ½ cup |
| 2 | Whisky measures | 2 | 2 |
| 2 | Dessert pears | 2 | 2 |
| 4 tbsp | Cranberry sauce | 4 tbsp | ⅓ cup |
| 150 ml | Double cream | ¼ pt | ½ cup |

1. Make the sauce.
2. Gently melt the butter in a pan.
3. Season the cutlets with salt and pepper. Add to the pan and fry slowly, turning them several times and cooking for about 10 minutes.
4. Pour the whisky over the cooked cutlets and ignite.
5. Add the game sauce and cook for 5 minutes.
6. Peel, halve and core the pears, and fill with cranberry sauce.
7. Just before serving, add the cream to the sauce. Heat gently but do not boil.
8. Serve the cutlets coated with the game sauce and garnished with the pears.

**Game sauce**

| Metric | | lb/oz | U.S.A. |
|---|---|---|---|
| 1 | Pheasant carcass | 1 | 1 |
| 1 tbsp | Oil | 1 tbsp | 1 tbsp |
| 2 | Shallots, coarsely chopped | 2 | ½ cup |
| 2 | Parsley stalks, coarsely chopped | 2 | 2 |
| 1 | Garlic clove, crushed | 1 | 1 |
| 1 | Thyme sprig | 1 | 1 |
| 1 | Bay leaf | 1 | 1 |
| 300 ml | Red wine | ½ pt | 1 cup |
| 300 ml | Demi-glace sauce | ½ pt | 1 cup |

1. Make the demi-glace sauce (opposite), then heat the oil in a large pan and fry the shallots and parsley until golden brown.
2. Add the garlic, thyme, bay leaf and red wine. Boil until the liquid is reduced to one quarter of its volume.
3. Add the demi-glace sauce and cook gently for 20 minutes.
4. Crush the carcass as finely as possible, then add to the sauce. Cook for a few minutes longer, then strain, season to taste, and keep warm.

55

## Demi-glace sauce

To make a demi-glace sauce, put equal quantities of Espagnole sauce (below) and strong beef stock into a heavy pan (with a few mushrooms). Simmer until the sauce is reduced by at least half. Remove, strain and re-heat. Remove from the heat and stir in a little dry sherry.

A VICTORIAN EXTRAVAGANZA (above) This amazing example of Victorian industrial architecture may be spotted en route to Chipping Norton – but for how long?

BARREL TOMBS, BURFORD CHURCH (left) If time permits, have a look at these unusual tombs in Burford Church – which is the second largest in Oxfordshire with a most impressive spire.

## Espagnole sauce

| Metric | | lb/oz | U.S.A. |
|---|---|---|---|
| 25 g | Ham or bacon (raw), chopped | 1 tbsp | 1 tbsp |
| 30 g | Butter | 1 oz | 1 tbsp |
| 1 | Carrot, peeled and chopped | 1 | 1 |
| 1 | Onion, chopped | 1 | 1 |
| 3 tbsp | Mushroom stalks, chopped | 3 tbsp | ⅓ cup |
| 2 tbsp | Celery, chopped (optional) | 2 tbsp | ¼ cup |
| 1 | Beef stock cube | 1 | 1 |
| 45 g | Flour | 1½ oz | ¼ cup |
| 2 tbsp | Tomato paste | 2 tbsp | ¼ cup |
| 250 g | Tomatoes, peeled and chopped | 8 oz | 2 cups |
| 1 tsp | Thyme | 1 tsp | 1 tsp |
| 1 | Bay leaf | 1 | 1 |

1. Cook the bacon in the butter for a few minutes.
2. Add the vegetables and sauté gently for 5 – 8 minutes.
3. Make a stock with the cube and 300 ml (½ pt) boiling water. Set aside.
4. Stir the flour into the vegetable mixture. Continue stirring until the flour browns well, then add the stock very gradually, stirring continuously.
5. When the sauce has thickened, stir in the tomato paste, tomatoes, thyme and bay leaf. Season lightly.
6. Simmer for 30 minutes, stirring occasionally and skimming off excess fat. Taste and correct the seasoning.
7. Strain the sauce into a basin and cover the surface with damp greaseproof or clingwrap to stop a skin forming.

## SMOKED SALMON ROULADE
*Serves 4*

Packs of relatively inexpensive smoked salmon pieces are now readily available at most freezer centres. Use them to make this light and tasty dish from the Rose Tree Restaurant on the riverside at Bourton-on-the-Water.

| Metric | | lb/oz | U.S.A. |
|---|---|---|---|
| 500 g | Smoked salmon pieces | 1 lb | 1 lb |
| 4 | Eggs, separated | 4 | 4 |
| 1 tbsp | Sherry | 1 tbsp | 1 tbsp |
| 2 tsp | Worcestershire sauce | 2 tsp | 2 tsp |
| 1 | Lemon, juice of | 1 | 1 |
| | For the filling: | | |
| 125 g | Cream cheese | 4 oz | ½ cup |
| 1 tbsp | Fresh parsley and lovage, chopped | 1 tbsp | 1 tbsp |
| 2 tbsp | Double cream | 2 tbsp | 2 tbsp |

### MOTOR MUSEUM

Car enthusiasts will enjoy visiting the motor museum housed in an old mill at Bourton-on-the-Water, and train buffs will appreciate the large model railway. Nature lovers should watch out for the dovecotes nestling in a wall in Sherborne Street.

## BOURTON-ON-THE-WATER

Spanned by a series of ornamental bridges, the River Windrush flows through Bourton-on-the-Water. Lying just off the Roman Fosse Way, this town boasts many beautiful buildings including an unusual church which combines a 14th century chancel and a Georgian tower with a Victorian nave.

1. Set the oven to 210°C, 425°F, Gas Mark 7.
2. Chop half the smoked salmon pieces finely. Blend them with the egg yolks, sherry, Worcestershire sauce and lemon juice.
3. Whip the egg whites until stiff and fold in the salmon mixture.
4. Put in a swiss roll tin lined with greased greaseproof paper, and bake in a hot oven for 10-15 minutes until lightly cooked. Do not over cook.
5. Place a clean tea towel over a cake rack and turn the roulade out on to the towel. Leave to cool.
6. To make the filling, blend the cream cheese with the herbs. Whip the cream and fold it in.
7. Peel the lining paper off the roulade and place the remaining salmon pieces on top. Spread on the filling and roll up. Slice, and serve with a salad.

## CRAB-STUFFED BIBURY TROUT
## WITH PRAWN SAUCE                                    *Serves 4*

Fishing in the crystal clear River Coln is a popular activity around Bibury, and visitors to the Swan Hotel can spy trout in the stream which runs through the hotel garden.

| Metric | | lb/oz | U.S.A. |
|---|---|---|---|
| | 4 × 400 g (14 oz) Trout | | |
| | Prawn sauce | | |
| 125 g | White crabmeat | 4 oz | ⅔ cup |
| 1 tbsp | Dry white wine | 1 tbsp | 1 tbsp |
| 1 tbsp | Lemon juice | 1 tbsp | 1 tbsp |
| ½ tbsp | Tomato purée | ½ tbsp | ½ tbsp |
| | Paprika | | |
| 1 tbsp | Double cream | 1 tbsp | 1 tbsp |

1. Wash and clean the trout and place in a shallow pan. Cover with water and poach gently for 30 minutes or until cooked. Meanwhile, make the prawn sauce.
2. Remove skin and bones carefully with a sharp knife, keeping fillets whole. Place on a warmed dish and keep hot.
3. Put the crabmeat, wine and lemon juice in a small pan and bring slowly to the boil. Reduce the heat and add the tomato purée. Season with salt and paprika to taste.
4. Add the cream and stir until thickened, but do not boil.
5. Place a little of the crabmeat mixture inside each "trout". Cover with the prawn sauce and serve immediately.

**Prawn sauce**

| Metric | | lb/oz | U.S.A. |
|---|---|---|---|
| | Fish skin and bones | | |
| 150 ml | White wine | ¼ pt | ½ cup |
| 1 | Bayleaf | 1 | 1 |
| 5-6 | Peppercorns | 5-6 | 5-6 |
| 40 g | Butter | 1 ½ oz | ¼ cup |
| 40 g | Flour | 1 ½ oz | ⅓ cup |
| 60 g | Tomato purée | 2 oz | 2 tbsp |
| 125 g | North Atlantic prawns | 4 oz | ⅔ cup |

1. Place the skin and bones in a large pan and cover with water (900 ml, 1 ½ pt, 3 cups). Add the wine, bay leaf and peppercorns. Bring to the boil then simmer for 30 minutes.
2. Melt the butter in a pan over a gentle heat and stir in the flour to make a roux. Cook for a few minutes.
3. Slowly add the fish stock, season with salt and pepper to taste and stir until smooth and simmering. Add the tomato purée. Peel the prawns and stir in just before serving.

*"Some circumstantial evidence is very strong,*
*as when you find a trout in the milk."*                    Miscellanies
                                                H.D. THOREAU, 1817-1862

## BOURTON-ON-THE-HILL

Climb the hill for a closer look at the 18th century stone built inn — The Horse and Groom. Pause for breath on the way up and admire the attractive terraces of 17th and 18th century cottages. Do not miss the golden stone church which houses the beautiful bell-metal Winchester Bushel and Peck. Dated 1816, they were used by local magistrates in the settlement of disputes — most often those involving the payment of tithes.

# Desserts & Teatime Treats

## DULCIA DOMESTICA

Serves 4-6

David Gilbert, of the Kings Head Hotel at Cirencester, has revealed how to make this sweet and tasty delicacy.

| Metric | | lb/oz | U.S.A. |
|---|---|---|---|
| 375 g | Stoned dates | 12 oz | ¾ lb |
| 60 g | Almonds, chopped | 2 oz | ⅔ cup |
| | Salt | | |
| 1-2 tsp | Butter | ¼ oz | 1-2 tsp |
| 1 tbsp | Honey | 1 tbsp | 1 tbsp |

1. Remove the stones from the dates with a sharp knife, being careful to keep the dates whole.
2. Stuff the dates with the nuts and roll them in the salt.
3. Melt the butter in a small, heavy saucepan, add the honey and gently bring to the boil.
4. Fry the dates in the mixture and serve immediately.

## BUTTERSCOTCH TART

Serves 6-8

Anyone with a sweet tooth will love this rich creation. It comes from Chef Hill of the Lygon Arms, Broadway.

| Metric | | lb/oz | U.S.A. |
|---|---|---|---|
| 225 g | Flour | 8 oz | 2 cups |
| 60 g | Butter | 2 oz | ¼ cup |
| 60 g | Lard | 2 oz | ¼ cup |
| 60 g | Caster sugar | 2 oz | ¼ cup |
| 1 | Egg, beaten | 1 | 1 |
| 300 ml | Double cream | ½ pt | 1 cup |
| 4 | Egg whites, beaten | 4 | 4 |

PENGUINS, FLAMINGOES, macaws, toucans and other exotic species can be seen thriving at Birdland, which lies in the grounds of a 16th century house near Bourton-on-the-Water.

| 2 tbsp | Grated chocolate | 2 tbsp | 2 tbsp |
| | For the filling: | | |
| 125 g | Butter | 4 oz | ½ cup |
| 500 g | Demerara sugar | 1 lb | 3 cups |
| 3 tbsp | Cornflour | 3 tbsp | ¼ cup |
| 300 ml | Condensed milk | ½ pt | 1 cup |
| 8 | Egg yolks | 8 | 8 |

1. Set the oven to 200°C, 400°F, Gas Mark 6.
2. To make the pastry, put the flour into a bowl with a pinch of salt and rub in the fats until the mixture resembles fine breadcrumbs. Stir in the caster sugar and beaten egg and mix to a soft dough. Roll out the pastry on a floured board and line a greased 25 cm (10") flan tin. Bake blind for 20-30 minutes.
3. To make the filling, melt the butter in a large pan and add the sugar. Dissolve the sugar, then bring to the boil to caramelize. Boil until the caramel is a light brown colour (if it becomes too brown it will be bitter).
4. Remove from the heat and add 600 ml (1 pt, 2½ cups) of boiling water. **This must be done very carefully as the caramel will spit.** Stir until the caramel has dissolved.
5. Mix the cornflour with a little condensed milk until smooth. Pour the remaining milk into a second pan and bring to the boil. Thicken with the cornflour, stirring all the time.
6. Continuing to stir, pour into the caramel and reboil until the mixture thickens. Add yolks (still stirring) and bring back to the boil. Remove from heat and sieve into the flan case.
7. Whisk the cream until thick and fold in the beaten egg whites. Spoon over the caramel and top with chocolate.

## RICH LEMON TART                                      Serves 6

A melt-in-the-mouth dessert which is equally nice hot or cold, from the Market House, Moreton-in-Marsh.

| Metric | | lb/oz | U.S.A. |
|---|---|---|---|
| 275 g | Shortcrust pastry | 10 oz | 10 oz |
| 300 ml | Double cream | ½ pt | 1 cup |
| 4 | Egg yolks | 4 | 4 |
| 125 g | Caster sugar | 4 oz | ½ cup |
| 60 g | Ground almonds | 2 oz | ½ cup |
| 125 g | Unsalted butter, softened | 4 oz | ½ cup |
| 2 | Lemons | 2 | 2 |

1. Set the oven to 170°C, 325°F, Gas Mark 3.
2. Line one 24 cm (9½") flan tin or two 18 cm (7") flan tins with pastry. Whip half the cream, and reserve.
3. Beat together the egg yolks and sugar, stir in the almonds, butter, remaining cream, the juice of both lemons and finely grated rind of one. Beat until smooth.
4. Pour into the pastry case and bake for about 40 minutes until golden brown. Serve with the whipped cream.

## GINGER AND ADVOCAAT SYLLABUB                    *Serves 4*

The Cotswold House Hotel at Chipping Campden overlooks a
large walled garden and is set in an imposing Regency house
with a fine early nineteenth century staircase. Their unusual
variation on an old English recipe is extravagant but worth it!

| Metric | | lb/oz | U.S.A. |
|---|---|---|---|
| 600 ml | *Double cream* | 1 pt | 2½ cups |
| 150 ml | *Advocaat* | ¼ pt | ½ cup |
| 125 ml | *Wine glass of ginger wine* | 4 fl oz | ½ cup |
| | *Several pieces of preserved ginger, chopped* | | |
| 4 | *Ginger biscuits* | 4 | 4 |
| | To decorate: | | |
| 30 g | *Walnuts, chopped* | 1 oz | ⅓ cup |

1. Whip the cream stiffly and stir in the advocaat and ginger
   wine.
2. Add the preserved ginger chopped into small pieces,
   reserving a little for decoration.
3. Place a ginger biscuit in the bottom of each of four glass
   dishes and pile the cream mixture on top.
4. Decorate with the reserved ginger and walnuts.

**Variation** Use ginger marmalade instead of ginger wine and
preserved ginger.

## COFFEE DIPLOMAT                                 *Serves 6*

A mouthwatering coffee and cream contribution from The
Manor in Lower Slaughter village.

| Metric | | lb/oz | U.S.A. |
|---|---|---|---|
| 30 | *Sponge finger biscuits** | 30 | 30 |
| 75 ml | *Milk* | ⅛ pt | ¼ cup |
| 4 tbsp | *Tia Maria* | 4 tbsp | ⅓ cup |
| 1 tbsp | *Instant coffee* | 1 tbsp | 1 tbsp |
| 600 ml | *Whipping Cream* | 1 pt | 2½ cups |
| 125 g | *Caster sugar* | 4 oz | ½ cup |
| 60 g | *Almonds, chopped* | 2 oz | ⅔ cup |

1. Soak half the sponge fingers in a little milk, then place
   them in a well-greased, loose-bottomed cake tin. Sprinkle
   with half the Tia Maria.
2. Mix the instant coffee to a strong essence with a small
   amount of hot water and allow to cool. Whip the cream
   until stiff, then fold in the essence and re-whip.
3. Spread half the cream over the sponge fingers and add
   another layer of sponge fingers. Sprinkle with the
   remaining Tia Maria and spread over the remaining cream.

4. Put the sugar in a heavy based pan with 2 tbsp water and heat until the sugar has dissolved. Bring to the boil gently until golden. Do not allow the caramel to boil too long or it will taste bitter.
5. Stir in the almonds and pour the caramel on to a greased metal baking tray. Allow to cool. When cold, break into small pieces and sprinkle over the top of the gateau.
6. Place in the freezer. Remove an hour before required, and ease out of the tin just before serving.

*A 75 g, 2½ oz packet contains 18 —Editor.

## GATEAU AU FROMAGE JAMAIQUE                    Serves 5-6

Rum-soaked raisins add an exotic touch to this dessert from the Old Manse Hotel, Bourton-on-the-Water.

| Metric | | lb/oz | U.S.A. |
|---|---|---|---|
| | For the biscuit base: | | |
| 11 | Digestive biscuits* | 11 | 11 |
| 60 g | Butter | 2 oz | ¼ cup |
| 1 tsp | Mixed spice | 1 tsp | 1 tsp |
| | For the filling: | | |
| 250 g | Philadelphia cheese | 9 oz | 9 oz |
| 400 g | Condensed milk, can of | 14 oz | 14 oz |
| 75 ml | Lemon juice | 2 fl oz | ¼ cup |
| 125 g | Raisins | 4 oz | ⅔ cup |
| 1 | Rum, measure of | 1 | 1 |
| | For the pineapple topping: | | |
| 1 tsp | Cornflour | 1 tsp | 1 tsp |
| 150 ml | Pineapple juice | ¼ pt | ½ cup |
| 250 g | Fresh pineapple, finely diced | 8 oz | 1½ cups |
| | Sugar to taste | | |

1. Soak the raisins in the rum for a few hours, but overnight if possible.
2. Place the biscuits in a polythene bag, tie the end, then crush with a rolling pin.
3. Melt the butter and stir in the crumbs and mixed spice. Spread 1 cm (½") thick, over a 25 cm (10") flan dish or plate and put in a cool place to set.
4. Place the cheese and milk in a china bowl and beat until smooth and creamy. Add the lemon juice and mix well.
5. Fold raisins and rum into cheese and pour over the base.
6. Slake the cornflour with 1 tsp pineapple juice. Heat the remaining juice with the pineapple. When hot, stir in the cornflour and cook gently until the mixture has thickened. Sweeten to taste, then allow to cool.
7. Spoon the pineapple topping on the centre of the cheesecake and refrigerate.

*175 g, 6 oz, 1½ cups — Editor.

## HONEY AND WALNUT ROULADE
*Serves 4*

On the river's edge at Bourton-on-the-Water is the Rose Tree Restaurant. Jane Mann has contributed her recipe for this light and luscious dessert.

| Metric | | lb/oz | U.S.A. |
|--------|--------|-------|--------|
| 4 | Eggs | 4 | 4 |
| 125 g | Caster sugar | 4 oz | ½ cup |
| 90 g | Walnuts, chopped | 3 oz | 1 cup |
| 60 g | Flour, sifted | 2 oz | ¼ cup |
| 3 tbsp | Runny honey | 3 tbsp | ¼ cup |
| 300 ml | Double cream | ½ pt | 1 cup |
| 2 tbsp | Icing sugar | 2 tbsp | 2 tbsp |

1. Grease and line a swiss roll tin and pre-heat the oven to 220°C, 450°F, Gas Mark 8.
2. Beat the eggs and sugar together with an electric mixer until they stand in peaks.
3. Mix the nuts and flour together, then fold into the whipped eggs with the honey.
4. Place in the prepared tin, and bake until risen and just firm. Do not overcook.
5. Place a tea towel on a wire rack and turn the cake out of the tin to cool.
6. Whip the cream and reserve a little for decoration. When the cake is completely cold, remove the paper then spread on the rest of the cream and roll the roulade up.
7. Pipe with cream and dust with icing sugar.

## PASSION FRUIT AND FRESH LIME SOUFFLE
*Serves 4*

For a light and tangy result, follow this Rose Tree recipe for an exotic soufflé.

| Metric | | lb/oz | U.S.A. |
|--------|--------|-------|--------|
| 3 | Limes*, grated rind and juice | 3 | 3 |
| 1 pkt | Gelatine | 1 pkt | 1 pkt |
| 4 | Passion fruit | 4 | 4 |
| 4 | Eggs | 4 | 4 |
| 175 g | Caster sugar | 6 oz | ¾ cup |
| 300 ml | Whipping cream | ½ pt | 1 cup |

*Two lemons may be substituted if limes are not available — Editor.

1. Warm the lime juice and melt the gelatine in it but do not allow the liquid to boil. Remove from the heat and add the rind and passion fruit pulp.
2. Place the eggs in a bowl with the caster sugar and whip with an electric mixer until stiff and very bulky.
3. Whip the cream and fold into the eggs with the lime mixture. Leave in a cool place to set.

## THE MODEL VILLAGE

No, you are not imagining things! This replica of Bourton-on-the-Water adjoining the Old New Inn, which has belonged to the Morris family for over fifty years, is exactly one ninth of the size of the original. Built from Cotswold stone, it makes an attractive and fascinating scene, welcoming visitors daily.

## JAMAICAN RUM SURPRISE                                    *Serves 4*

A quick and easy recipe from the George Hotel, Shipston-on-Stour.

| Metric | | lb/oz | U.S.A. |
|---|---|---|---|
| | Plain sponge cake | | |
| 1 can | Sliced pears (600 g, 20 oz) | 1 can | 1 can |
| 300 ml | Double cream | ½ pt | 1 cup |
| 2 tbsp | Rum | 2 tbsp | 2 tbsp |
| 2 | Bananas, sliced | 2 | 2 |
| | To decorate: | | |
| | Grated chocolate or | | |
| | chopped glacé cherries | | |

1. Place small pieces of plain sponge in the bottom of four wine glasses.
2. Drain the juice from the pears. Pour a little over the sponge pieces — just enough to moisten.
3. Whip the cream with the rum until almost thick then stir in the fruit. Spoon into the glasses and refrigerate.
4. Before serving, sprinkle with grated chocolate or top with glacé cherries.

## CHARLOTTE ROYALE

An aptly named recipe from Chipping Campden's oldest inn, the Noel Arms — it is recorded that Charles II stayed there in 1651.

| Metric | | lb/oz | U.S.A. |
|---|---|---|---|
| 175 g | Caster sugar | 6 oz | ¾ cup |
| 6 | Eggs | 6 | 6 |
| 175 g | Plain flour, sieved | 6 oz | 1½ cups |
| 60 g | Butter | 2 oz | ¼ cup |
| | Caster sugar, to sprinkle | | |
| 125 g | Strawberry jam | 4 oz | ⅓ cup |
| | Bavarois | | |

1. Set the oven to 200°C, 400°F, Gas Mark 6. Grease and line two swiss roll tins with greased greaseproof paper.
2. Lay a sheet of tin foil over a baking tray and place the sugar in the centre. Put the tray in the oven to warm the sugar.
3. Break the eggs into a mixing bowl and whisk well. When there is a slight ring of caramel around the outside of the sugar, add to the eggs. Set your electric mixer to top speed and whisk until the mixture is light and the whisk leaves a trail.
4. Gently fold in the flour with a wooden spatula. When the flour is all mixed in, melt the butter and add to the mixture. Stir well.
5. Pour the mixture into the prepared tins, spreading it very thinly, about 1 cm (½") thick, and bake in the oven for about 8 minutes until golden brown.
6. Remove and slide the sponge out of the tin. Sprinkle with sugar and cover with a dry tea towel until slightly cooled.
7. Turn the sponge over, and while still warm, remove the greaseproof paper and trim off 1 cm (½") all around the edge (it will then roll without cracking). Spread gently with jam and roll into a swiss roll. Cut into thin slices and place in a greased soufflé or bavarois mould.

### Bavarois

| Metric | | lb/oz | U.S.A. |
|---|---|---|---|
| 60 g | Sugar | 2 oz | ¼ cup |
| 4 | Eggs, separated | 4 | 4 |
| 3 | Gelatine leaves* | 3 | 3 |
| 300 ml | Double cream | ½ pt | 1 cup |
| 600 ml | Milk | 1 pt | 2½ cups |
| ½ tsp | Vanilla essence | ½ tsp | ½ tsp |

1. Place the sugar and egg yolks in a bowl and whisk well.
2. Soak the leaf gelatine in 1 tbsp cold water. Whip the double cream until it is thick. Place the egg whites in another bowl and whisk until they are stiff and stand in peaks.

3. Put the milk in a pan and bring to the boil. Pour the boiling milk on to the eggs and sugar and whisk well. Add the vanilla essence. Now you have a *sauce anglaise*.
4. Place ice cubes in a large bowl and stand the bowl with the sauce anglaise on top of the ice to cool quickly.
5. Spoon the gelatine into the warm mixture and stir until it is dissolved.
6. When nearing setting point, fold in the egg whites and half the whipped cream, reserving the remainder for decoration. Just as the bavarois is setting pour into the dish lined with the swiss rolls.
7. Chill overnight until set, turn out and decorate with the reserved whipped cream.

*\* Powdered gelatine (30g, 1oz) dissolved in warm water can be used in place of leaf gelatine — Editor.*

## BAKED ALMOND AND PEACH CHEESECAKE        *Serves 6*

Cheesecakes are universally popular. This one owes its lightness to being made with a mixture of cream and cottage cheese. The recipe comes from the Island House Restaurant, Chipping Campden.

| *Metric* | | *lb/oz* | *U.S.A.* |
|---|---|---|---|
| 175 g | *Digestive biscuits, crushed* | 6 oz | 1 ½ cups |
| 80 g | *Butter, melted* | 3 oz | ½ cup |
| 1 tsp | *Ground cinnamon* | 1 tsp | 1 tsp |
| 125 g | *Sugar* | 4 oz | ½ cup |
| 2 | *Eggs, lightly beaten* | 2 | 2 |
| ½ | *Lemon, grated rind and juice* | ½ | ½ |
| 150 ml | *Single cream* | 4 fl. oz. | ½ cup |
| 225 g | *Cottage cheese* | 8 oz | 1 cup |
| 125 g | *Ground almonds* | 4 oz | 1 cup |
| 2 | *Peaches, sliced* | 2 | 2 |

1. Set the oven to 180°C, 350°F, Gas Mark 4, and lightly grease a 20 cm (8") shallow, loose-bottomed cake tin.
2. Mix the biscuit crumbs well with the melted butter, cinnamon and half the sugar. Reserve 2 tbsp and press the remainder evenly in the tin base. Refrigerate.
3. Combine the eggs, remaining sugar, ¼ tsp salt and the lemon rind and juice. Beat until well blended.
4. Stir in the cream, cottage cheese and nuts, and pour the mixture into the lined cake tin. Sprinkle the remaining crumb mixture on top and bake until the filling has set, about 35-45 minutes. A skewer inserted into the centre should come out clean.
5. Turn off the heat and leave in the oven for a further 10 minutes with the door open, then remove and allow to cool at room temperature. Top with peaches and serve cold.

## CHOCOLATE BRANDY REFRIGERATOR CAKE  *Serves 8-10*

Apart from melting the chocolate, no cooking is involved in the preparation of this rich and popular dessert from the Old New Inn, Bourton-on-the-Water.

| Metric | | lb/oz | U.S.A. |
|---|---|---|---|
| 225 g | Digestive biscuits | 8 oz | 2 cups |
| 225 g | Plain chocolate | 8 oz | 8 squares |
| 225 g | Butter | 8 oz | 1 cup |
| 2 | Eggs | 2 | 2 |
| 85 g | Caster sugar | 3 oz | ⅓ cup |
| 60 g | Glacé cherries, chopped | 2 oz | ¼ cup |
| 60 g | Walnut halves | 2 oz | ½ cup |
| 3-4 tbsp | Brandy | 3-4 tbsp | ¼ cup |

1. To prepare the biscuits, put them into a clean strong plastic bag then crush them coarsely with a rolling pin.

2. Melt the chocolate and butter *gently* in a basin over a pan of boiling water on a low heat.
3. Whisk the eggs and sugar together until light and creamy. Fold in the chocolate mixture.
4. Fold in the cherries and walnuts (reserving four of each), and the crushed biscuits. Add the brandy and stir well.
5. Put into a greased bread or cake tin and leave in the refrigerator for 3-4 hours.
6. Turn out on to a serving dish and decorate the top, alternating cherries and walnuts.

## STRAWBERRY SHORTCAKE  *Serves 6*

This recipe for a traditional English summer dessert comes from the Old Kings Arms Pantry, Chipping Campden.

| Metric | | lb/oz | U.S.A. |
|---|---|---|---|
| 225 g | Plain flour | 8 oz | 2 cups |
| ½ tsp | Bicarbonate of soda | ½ tsp | ½ tsp |
| 1 tsp | Cream of tartar | 1 tsp | 1 tsp |
| 60 g | Butter | 2 oz | ¼ cup |
| 45 g | Caster sugar | 1½ oz | ¼ cup |
| 1 | Egg, beaten | 1 | 1 |
| 3-4 tbsp | Milk | 3-4 tbsp | ¼ cup |

For the filling:

| | | | |
|---|---|---|---|
| 250 g | *Strawberries* | 8 oz | ½ lb |
| 300 ml | *Double cream* | ½ pt | 1 cup |
| 1 tbsp | *Milk* | 1 tbsp | 1 tbsp |
| 1 tbsp | *Caster sugar, or to taste* | 1 tbsp | 1 tbsp |
| 60 g | *Butter* | 2 oz | ¼ cup |

1. Set the oven to 210°C, 425°F, Gas Mark 7.
2. Sift the flour, bicarbonate of soda and a pinch of salt into a bowl. Stir in the cream of tartar.
3. Cut the butter into pieces and rub into the flour until the mixture resembles fine breadcrumbs, then blend in the sugar.
4. Make a well in the centre, stir in the egg and add enough milk to give a manageable dough.
5. Knead lightly on a floured surface, then roll the dough into an 18 cm (7") circle.
6. Place on a greased baking tray, dust lightly with flour, and bake on the top shelf of the oven for 20 minutes.
7. Remove from the oven and cool on a wire rack.
8. For the filling, wash, hull and slice the strawberries thickly. Whisk together the cream and milk with sugar to taste, until the cream is thick and holds its shape.
9. Cut the shortcake into three layers horizontally and spread each layer with butter.
10. Reserve a little cream for decoration then spread the remainder on the layers. Top each one with strawberries, sandwich together and decorate with piped cream.

VISIT THE ENCHANTING VILLAGE OF LOWER SLAUGHTER and spot the yew-trimmed window (left) and the old trough.

FRANGIPANS                                    *Makes about 20*

These light and crunchy jam and almond tartlets may be sampled at the Market House, Moreton-in-Marsh, which provided this easy-to-follow recipe.

| Metric |  | lb/oz | U.S.A. |
|---|---|---|---|
| 125 g | Butter, softened | 4 oz | ½ cup |
| 125 g | Caster sugar | 4 oz | ½ cup |
| 1 | Egg, beaten | 1 | 1 |
| 125 g | Ground almonds | 4 oz | 1 cup |
| 30 g | Plain flour | 1 oz | 2 tbsp |
| 3 tsp | Lemon juice | 3 tsp | 4 tsp |
|  | Almond essence |  |  |
| 225 g | Shortcrust pastry | 8 oz | ½ lb |
| 125 g | Jam | 4 oz | ⅓ cup |
| 60 g | Flaked almonds | 2 oz | ½ cup |
| 10 | Glacé cherries | 10 | 10 |

1. Set the oven to 150°C, 300°F, Gas Mark 2.
2. Beat the butter and sugar together until light and fluffy.
3. Add the egg a little at a time, alternating with the ground almonds and the flour. Add the lemon juice and almond essence.
4. Lightly grease about 20 small patty tins. Roll out the pastry on a floured board and line the patty tins.
5. Drop a little jam in the bottom of each pastry case then place a good teaspoonful of the almond mixture on top.
6. Top each with a few flaked almonds and bake for 35-40 minutes until risen and golden brown.
7. Brush with a little warmed jam and top each frangipan with half a cherry.

CHOCOLATE ORANGE CAKE

A sure and simple recipe from the Market House Restaurant, Moreton-in-Marsh.

| Metric |  | lb/oz | U.S.A. |
|---|---|---|---|
| 2 tbsp | Milk | 2 tbsp | 2 tbsp |
| 4 tbsp | Cocoa powder | 4 tbsp | ⅓ cup |
| 250 g | Self raising flour | 9 oz | 2 cups |
| 2 tsp | Baking powder | 2 tsp | 2 tsp |
| 225 g | Caster sugar | 8 oz | 1 cup |
| 225 g | Soft margarine | 8 oz | 1 cup |
| ½ | Orange, grated rind | ½ | ½ |
| 5 | Eggs, beaten | 5 | 5 |

1. Set the oven to 150°C, 300°F, Gas Mark 2.
2. Soften the cocoa powder with the milk (and with a little warm water if necessary).
3. Place all ingredients in a large bowl and whisk until smooth.

4. Divide the mixture between two 24 cm (9½") greased and lined sandwich tins. Bake for 35 minutes.
5. Remove from the tins and allow to cool.
6. Fill with butter icing and cover with fudge icing.

## Chocolate butter icing

| Metric | | lb/oz | U.S.A. |
|---|---|---|---|
| 60 g | Butter, softened | 2 oz | ¼ cup |
| 90 g | Icing sugar, sifted | 3 oz | ¾ cup |
| 1 tbsp | Cocoa powder | 1 tbsp | 1 tbsp |

1. Cream the butter and sugar together until light and fluffy.
2. Dissolve the cocoa in 1 tbsp of warm water. Beat very slowly into the butter and sugar. Refrigerate till needed.

## Chocolate fudge icing

| Metric | | lb/oz | U.S.A. |
|---|---|---|---|
| 300 g | Icing sugar, sifted | 10 oz | 2½ cups |
| 3 tbsp | Cocoa powder | 3 tbsp | ¼ cup |
| 65 g | Butter | 2½ oz | ⅓ cup |
| 2 tbsp | Milk | 2 tbsp | 2 tbsp |
| 1 tbsp | Golden syrup | 1 tbsp | 1 tbsp |

1. Mix the icing sugar and cocoa together.
2. Melt the butter in a small pan with the milk and golden syrup. Beat into the sugar and cocoa. **Use immediately as this icing sets very quickly.**

SOUS NUT                                            *Makes 24*

Children and adults alike will love these crunch-and-nut squares from St. Edward's Café, Stow-on-the-Wold, originally the home of a wealthy merchant. It is believed that the front of the building was constructed by the same craftsmen who built Blenheim Palace.

| Metric | | lb/oz | U.S.A. |
|---|---|---|---|
| 450 g | Cooking fat or lard | 1 lb | 2 cups |
| 200 g | Milk powder | 7 oz | 1¾ cups |
| 200 g | Desiccated coconut | 7 oz | 2⅓ cups |
| 90 g | Rice Krispies | 3 oz | 3 cups |
| 225 g | Sultanas | 8 oz | 1⅓ cups |
| 300 g | Icing sugar | 10 oz | 2½ cups |
| | A few cherries and strips of angelica, chopped | | |

1. Place the cooking fat in a saucepan and melt over a gentle heat. Do not allow to boil.
2. Put the remaining ingredients in a large bowl and stir well.
3. Pour the fat over the mixture and mix well.
4. Spoon the mixture into two ungreased oblong swiss roll tins and press down well. Allow to set in the refrigerator, then cut into squares.

## MADELEINES

These little coconut castles are popular in Shipston-on-Stour with visitors to the Kerry Tea Rooms.

| Metric | | lb/oz | U.S.A. |
|---|---|---|---|
| 125 g | *Butter* | 4 oz | ½ cup |
| 125 g | *Caster sugar* | 4 oz | ½ cup |
| 2 | *Eggs, beaten* | 2 | 2 |
| 125 g | *Self-raising flour* | 4 oz | 1 cup |
| 125 g | *Red jam* | 4 oz | ⅓ cup |
| 60 g | *Desiccated coconut* | 2 oz | ¾ cup |
| | *To decorate:* | | |
| | *Cherry halves and angelica* | | |
| | *leaves* | | |

1. Set the oven to 190°C, 375°F, Gas Mark 5. Grease and flour 12 dariole tins.
2. Place the butter in a large bowl and beat with a wooden spoon until soft. Add the sugar and beat until the mixture is pale and creamy.
3. Slowly beat the eggs into the mixture. Fold in the flour with a metal spoon.
4. Spoon into the tins, filling them three-quarters full. Stand the tins on a baking tray and bake for 20 minutes or until well risen and golden.
5. Remove from the oven and turn out on to a wire rack to cool. Trim a little off the wide end of each cake until they stand level.
6. Heat the jam until runny and brush it over the cakes.
7. Roll each cake in coconut, and top each with half a cherry and two angelica leaves.

THE KERRY TEA ROOMS brandy mincemeat and homemade jams make a perfect gift.

**Variations** Add a drop or two of almond essence to the mixture. Decorate by brushing with warmed lemon curd and rolling in chopped nuts. Or brush with warmed apricot jam and roll in chocolate vermicelli.

LOWER SLAUGHTER

Lying along both banks, Lower Slaughter is linked by a series of small bridges across the River Windrush. Tiny and very typical of a Cotswold village, it was the site of industry in 1452 when roofing slates for New College, Oxford were quarried here.

# Index

# MEASURES & CONVERSIONS

Please read the notes on measures and conversions on page 5.
The table below will help our American readers.

| English | American |
| --- | --- |
| Baking powder | Baking soda |
| Beetroot | Beets |
| Bicarbonate of soda | Baking soda |
| Caster sugar | Fine granulated sugar |
| Chicory | Endive |
| Courgettes | Zucchini |
| Cornflour | Cornstarch |
| Demerara sugar | Soft light brown sugar |
| Desiccated coconut | Shredded coconut |
| Digestive biscuits | Graham crackers |
| Double cream | Heavy cream |
| Flaked almonds | Slivered almonds |
| Gherkins | Baby dill pickles |
| Glacé cherries | Candied red cherries |
| Golden syrup | Light corn syrup |
| Grill | Broil |
| Icing sugar | Confectioners' sugar |
| Lard | White fat |
| Lemon curd | Lemon cheese |
| Plain chocolate | Semi-sweet chocolate |
| Redcurrant jelly | Cranberry jelly |
| Single cream | Light cream |
| Spring onions | Scallions |
| Streaky bacon rashers | Canadian bacon strips |
| Sultanas | Light raisins |
| Swedes | Rutabagas |
| Treacle | Molasses |

# RESTAURANTS & HOTELS

We would like to thank the following for their help and
generosity in giving us the recipes listed below. Local tele-
phone numbers are also provided.

BROADWAY HOTEL, The Green, Broadway                                852401
*Chef: Vernon Crowther*
  Salsify pasties, 16
  Curried pears, 18
  Fillets of pork Charlotte, 44
  Pheasant in port wine with savoury dumplings, 50
Luncheon: 12.15-2 pm. Dinner: 7-9 pm

BURY BARN INN, The Roundabout, Burford                               2236
*Chef: Michael Conway*
  Bury Barn chicken, 48
Open: normal pub hours.

**CENTURION ROOMS**, 103 Watermoor Road, Cirencester 2933
*Proprietors: Mr and Mrs T.W. Watson*
  Roast partridge papon, 52
Luncheon: 12-2 pm (Mon-Sat and
1st Sun in month)
Dinner: 7.30-10 pm (Mon, Wed-Sat)

**COTSWOLD HOUSE HOTEL**, The Square, Chipping Campden
*Chefs: Mr. G. Douglas and Miss L. Morton* 840330
  Ginger and advocaat syllabub, 62
Luncheon: 12.30-2 pm. Dinner: 7.30-9 pm

**FLEECE HOTEL**, Market Place, Cirencester 2680
*Chef: Bruce Buchan*
  Gloucester cheese soup, 10
Luncheon: 12.30-2 pm. Dinner: 7-9.30 pm

**FOSSE MANOR HOTEL**, The Fosseway, Stow-on-the-Wold 30354
*Proprietor: Mr R. Johnston*
*Chef: Mr. Smart*
  Barbecued spare ribs, 45
  Breast of chicken stuffed with prawns and smoked salmon, 49
Luncheon: 12.30-2.30 pm. Dinner: 7.30-9.30 pm (Mon-Fri) 10 pm (Sat)

**GALLERY RESTAURANT**, North Street, Broadway 853555
*Proprietress: Christine Hurst*
  Lamb kebabs, 35
Luncheon: 12-3 pm. Dinner 6.30-9.30 pm

**GEORGE HOTEL**, Shipston-on-Stour 61453
*Chef: Julian Lachkovic*
  Jamaican rum surprise, 65
Luncheon: 11-2.30 pm. Dinner: 6-11 pm

**GOBLETS WINE BAR**, High Street, Broadway 852255
*Chef: Betty Baylif*
  Mild mustard sausages, 47
  Minna's chicken, 47
Open: 11.30 am-2.30 pm. 11.30 am-11 pm (Fri-Sat)
Dinner: 6-9.30 pm (Mon-Sun)

**ISLAND HOUSE RESTAURANT**, High Street, Chipping Campden
*Chef: Andrew Porter* 840598
  Island House prawn cocktail, 26
  Sauté scampi mornay, 30
  Baked almond and peach cheesecake, 67
Luncheon: 12-2 pm. Dinner: 7-9 pm
Closed all day Thursday and Sunday evenings.

**KERRY TEA ROOMS**, Market Place, Shipston-on-Stour 61224
*Cooks: Mrs C. Gibbs and Mrs D. Smith*
  Madeleines, 72
Open: 9 am-5.30 pm (Mon-Sat)
3-6 pm Bank holiday Sunday and Monday

**KINGS ARMS HOTEL, Chipping Campden**     840256
*Chef: Mrs V.M. Willmot*
  Brandied chicken livers with oranges and cream, 18
  Roast rack of English lamb with cucumber and mint yogurt, 32
Bar snacks: 12.30-2 pm
Dinner: 7.30-9 pm. Sunday luncheon: 1-2 pm

**KINGS HEAD HOTEL, 2 Market Place, Cirencester**     3322
*Chef: David Gilbert*
  Patina de piscis fricta, 27
  Agninam excaldatam et conchichlam de pisa simplici, 38
  Dulcia domestica, 60
Dinner: 7-9.30 pm (Sun-Thur). 7-10 pm (Fri-Sat)
Sunday Luncheon: 12.30-2 pm

**LORDS OF THE MANOR HOTEL AND RESTAURANT,**
**Upper Slaughter**     20243
*Chefs: Anne Riley and Caroline Wrightson*
  Malmesbury pheasant with apples, 51
Luncheon: 12.30-2 pm. Dinner: 7.30-9.45 pm

**LYGON ARMS, Broadway**     852255
*Chef: Shaun Hill*
  Saffron soup, 11
  Venison with blood oranges, 53
  Butterscotch tart, 60
Luncheon: 12.30-2 pm. Dinner: 7.30-9.15 pm

**MARKET HOUSE, High Street, Moreton-in-Marsh**     50767
*Proprietors: Mr and Mrs M. Habgood*
  Rich lemon tart, 61
  Frangipans, 70
  Chocolate orange cake, 70
Open: 9.30 am-6 pm. Sunday Luncheon: 12-2 pm

**NOEL ARMS HOTEL, High Street, Chipping Campden**     840317
*Chef: John Thursfield*
  Charlotte Royale, 66
Luncheon: 12.30-2 pm. Dinner: 7-9 pm

**OLD KINGS ARMS PANTRY, High Street, Chipping Campden**
*Chef: Mrs Sandra Porter*     840826
  Strawberry shortcake, 68
Open: 10 am-6 pm (except Thursdays)
Dinner: 7-10 pm (Fri-Sat)

**OLD MANSE HOTEL, Bourton-on-the-Water**     20642
*Chef: Mr P. E. Vincent*
  Melon Madame Drummond Hay, 17
  Brochettes Benjamin, 33
  Gâteau au fromage Jamaique, 63
Luncheon: 12.30-1.45 pm
Dinner: 7.30-8.30 pm (Sun-Thur). 7.30-9.30 pm (Fri-Sat)

**OLD NEW INN, High Street, Bourton-on-the-Water**     20467
*Chef: Miss A. Colmer*
  Cold salmon and nut roll, 27
  Lamb portfolio, 34
  Lambs' kidneys in pepper and cream sauce, 37
  Chocolate brandy refrigerator cake, 68
Luncheon: 12.30-2.30 pm. Dinner: 7.30-8.30 pm

**RAFTERS**, Park Street, Stow-on-the-Wold                30200
*Proprietor/Chef: Keith Maby*
  Hot vegetable mousse with hazelnut sauce, 14
Luncheon: 12.15-2.15 pm (Mon-Sat)
Dinner: 7.15-10 pm (Mon-Sat)

**ROSE TREE**, Riverside, Bourton-on-the-Water                20635
*Proprietress chef: Jane Mann*
  Mussels in garlic and cheese, 30
  Smoked salmon roulade, 56
  Honey and walnut roulade, 64
  Passion fruit and fresh lime soufflé, 64
Dinner: 7.30-9.30 pm (Tues-Sat). Sunday luncheon: 12.30-2 pm

**ROYALIST HOTEL**, Digbeth Street, Stow-on-the-Wold                30670
*Cook: Liz Notram*
  Norwegian baked mushrooms, 12
  Entrecôte Russian, 39
Luncheon: 12-2 pm. Dinner: 7-9.30 pm

**SWAN HOTEL**, Bibury                204
*Chef: Kenneth Llewellyn*
  Attereau of tongue and mushrooms, 13
  Fish quenelles with lobster sauce, 28
  Gloucestershire escalôpes of pork with apricots, 44
  Spiced breast of chicken, 48
  Venison in whisky and game sauce, 54
  Crab-stuffed Bibury trout with prawn sauce, 58
Luncheon: 12.15-1.30 pm. Dinner: 7.15-8.30 pm

**ST EDWARDS CAFE**, The Square, Stow-on-the-Wold                30351
*Chef: Mr M. Neville*
  Sous nut, 71
Open: 9 am-5.30 pm

IT WAS AT DONNINGTON just 1½ miles north of Stow that Lord
Astley, with three thousand Royalist troops, surrendered to the
Parliamentarians on 21st March 1646, the final defeat of the bitter Civil
War. A monument at Naseby marks the battlefield. Cromwell
imprisoned a thousand Royalists in the 12th century Stow church.

**THE MANOR**, Lower Slaughter                20456
*Chef: John Gallagher*
  Scallops in bacon, 29
  Coffee diplomat, 62
Luncheon: 12.30-2 pm. Dinner: 7.30-9 pm

**WARREN OLDE WORLDE RESTAURANT**, Sherborne Street,   20271
Bourton-on-the-Water
*Chef: Mr B.J. Tanner*
  Pork Brion, 42
Open: 10 am-9.30 pm

**WHITE HART**, High Street, Chipping Norton                2572
*Chef: John Mawer*
  Mushrooms abbott, 12
Luncheon: 12.30-2 pm. Dinner: 7-9.30 pm

**WHITE HART ROYAL HOTEL**, High Street, Moreton-in-Marsh 50731
*Chef: Mr P.S. Witts*
  Potted Stilton cream with walnuts, 14
Dinner: 7-9.30 pm

## IS THAT A CAVALIER I SEE BEFORE ME?

Don't think you are necessarily seeing a ghost if you should spot a wandering Roundhead or a laughing Cavalier, like the happy fellow here. He is likely to be a member of The Sealed Knot, a society whose members spend their leisure hours enthusiastically re-enacting famous Civil War battles.

As he departs to fight another day, so must we! But we do so with a wish and a prayer — a wish that on your wanderings you will enjoy this and other books in the series, and a reminder of that lovely and timeless prayer attributed to Lord Anstey before the Battle of Edgehill:

*"O Lord! Thou knowest how busy I must be this day:
If I forget Thee, do not Thou forget me."*